Cambridge English
Advanced
Practice Tests

Four tests for the Cambridge English: Advanced exam

MARK HARRISON

OXFORD

UNIVERSITY PRESS

OXFORD
UNIVERSITY PRESS

Great Clarendon Street, Oxford, OX2 6DP, United Kingdom

Oxford University Press is a department of the University of Oxford. It furthers the University's objective of excellence in research, scholarship, and education by publishing worldwide. Oxford is a registered trade mark of Oxford University Press in the UK and in certain other countries

© Oxford University Press 2014

The moral rights of the author have been asserted

First published in 2014

2024

13

ISBN: 978 0 19 451267 1

Printed in China

This book is printed on paper from certified and well-managed sources

ACKNOWLEDGEMENTS

We would like to thank the following for kind permission to reproduce photographs:
Alamy pp.25 (motorway/Homer W Sykes), 25 (Bin/Alex Segre), 36 (IML Image Group Ltd), 39 (flycatcher/imagebroker), 47 (Jessye Norman/Lebrecht Music and Arts Photo Library), 47 (mechanics/vario images GmbH & Co.KG), 47 (driving/Stockbroker), 47 (Julia Mancuso/PCN Photography), 47 (Nathan Sykes/Chris Gibson), 58 (Andrew Catterall), 69 (Paramedics/ Jonathan Larsen/Diadem Images), 91 (hiker/Manfred Gottschalk), 91 (diver/ David Fleetham); Ardea p.39 (Red Kite/ Geoff Trinder); Arthur Lockwood p.61; Corbis UK Ltd. p.69 (family/Artiga Photo); Fotolia p.83 (KarenDMartin); Getty Images pp.17, 25 (cinema/ Emmanuel Faure), 47 (Cooking class), 47 (Michael Phelps), 69 (Actress/ WireImage), 69 (politician/2013 AFP), 69 (football team), 69 (businessman/ Tomaz Levstek), 91 (friends/Image Source), 91 (colleagues/Jupiter Images), 91 (tourists/Tim Hall), Oxford University Press p.32 (Laura Doss); Rex Features pp.25 (Cybermen/Alex Lentati/Evening Standard), 25 (Game of Thrones/c.HBO/ Everett), 47 (Gok Wan/Ken McKay); Ronald Grant Archive p.25 (Damages); Superstock Ltd. pp.39 (Dartford Warbler/NaturePL), 39 (Sea Eagle/age fotostock),

The author and publisher are grateful to those who have given permission to reproduce the following extracts and adaptations of copyright material: p.6 Adapted extract from "Taking photographs ruins the memory, research finds" by Sarah Knapton, *The Telegraph*, 10 December 2013 © Telegraph Media Group Limited 2013. Reproduced by permission. p.7 Adapted extract from "On the hunt for the best young female entrepreneurs" by Rebecca Burn-Callander, *The Telegraph*, 11 January 2014 © Telegraph Media Group Limited 2014. Reproduced by permission. p.8 Adapted extract from "Views of departing staff are valuable" by Caroline Cook, *Hendon and Finchley Times*, 10 July 2006. Reproduced by permission of Newsquest London Ltd. p.10 Adapted extract from "The Great Indoors: At Home in the Modern British House, by Ben Highmore, review" by Alwyn Turner, *The Telegraph*, 14 January 2014 © Telegraph Media Group Limited 2014. Reproduced by permission. p.14 Adapted extract from "Never turn your back on the sea" by Horatio Clare, *The Telegraph*, 1 January 2014 © Telegraph Media Group Limited 2014. Reproduced by permission. p.17 Adapted extract from "Deaf Children's Ad Hoc Language Evolves and Instructs" by Nicholas Wade from *The New York Times*, 21 September 2004 © 2004 The New York Times. All rights reserved. Used by permission and protected by the Copyright Laws of the United States. The printing, copying, redistribution, or transmission of this Content without express written permission is prohibited. p.20 Adapted extract from "Unaccustomed as I am…" by Rosemary Behan, *The Telegraph*, © Telegraph Media Group Limited. Reproduced by permission. p.20 Adapted extract from "Linking City with Suburbia" by Janaki Mahadevan, *Hendon and Finchley Times*, 2 November 2006. Reproduced by permission of Newsquest London Ltd. p.21 Adapted extract from "Tools of the Trade" by Rachel Carlyle, *The Telegraph*, © Telegraph Media Group Limited. Reproduced by permission. p.22 Adapted extract from "Go on, snigger all you like" by Rupert

Christiansen, *The Telegraph*, 24 October 2005 © Telegraph Media Group Limited 2005. Reproduced by permission. p.28 Adapted extract from "Tracey Curtis-Taylor: from Cape Town to Cairo in a Forties biplane" by Claire Cohen, *The Telegraph*, 11 January 2014 © Telegraph Media Group Limited 2014. Reproduced by permission. p.29 Adapted extract from "On track for a triple whammy" by Nicholas Roe, *The Telegraph* © Telegraph Media Group Limited. Reproduced by permission. p.32 Adapted extract from "Simply ticking the boxes isn't enough" by Dr. James Rieley, *The Telegraph*, 31 Mar 2005 © Telegraph Media Group Limited 2005. Reproduced by permission. p.36 Adapted extract from "John Craxton, Fitzwilliam Museum, review" by Richard Dorment, *The Telegraph*, 2 January 2014 © Telegraph Media Group Limited 2014. Reproduced by permission. p.39 Adapted extract from "Winged winners and losers" by Mark Cocker, *The Telegraph*, 20 August 2005. © Telegraph Media Group Limited. Reproduced by permission. p.44 Adapted extract from "Don't ask your nearest and dearest for advice. Find a fellow writer who can be a helpful critic" by Louise Doughty, *The Telegraph* © Telegraph Media Group Limited. Reproduced by permission. p.45 Adapted extract from "24 Hours in Food" by Kate Salter, *Stella Magazine* © Telegraph Media Group Limited. Reproduced by permission. p.45 Adapted extract from "OK, who's got all the teaspoons?" by Maya Kessler, *The Telegraph*, 21 November 2006 © Telegraph Media Group Limited 2006. Reproduced by permission. p.50 Adapted extract from "The man who showed us the world" by Eric Owen, *The Telegraph* © Telegraph Media Group Limited. Reproduced by permission. p.51 Adapted extract from "Bits of History (of Bits) On the Auction Block" by Katie Hafner from *The New York Times*, 17 February 2005 © 2005 The New York Times. All rights reserved. Used by permission and protected by the Copyright Laws of the United States. The printing, copying, redistribution, or transmission of this Content without express written permission is prohibited. p.52 Adapted extract from "Alicia Rhett – obituary", *The Telegraph*, 7 January 2014 © Telegraph Media Group Limited 2014. Reproduced by permission. p.54 Extract from *Brick Lane* by Monica Ali, published by Doubleday. Reprinted with the permission of The Random House Group Limited, Abner Stein Ltd and Scribner Publishing Group. Copyright © 2003 by Monica Ali. All rights reserved. p.58 Adapted extract from "The most significant experience of my youth was singing in a choir" by Michael White, *The Telegraph*, 5 December 2013 © Telegraph Media Group Limited 2013. Reproduced by permission. p.61 Adapted extract from "Art: The Right Stripes" by Frank Whitford, *The Sunday Times*, 4 September 2005. Reproduced by kind permission. p.64 Adapted extract from "The Workout" by Sam Murphy, *Hydro Active Women's Challenge*, 2006. Reproduced by permission of London Marathon Limited. p.65 Adapted extract from "I'll tell you what I want, what I really, really want" by Joanne Silverstein, *East Finchley Guide*, May 2006. Reproduced by kind permission. p.66 Adapted extract from "Invisible benefits" by Sian Griffiths, *The Sunday Times*, 30 October 2005. Reproduced by permission of News Syndication. p.72 Adapted extract from "High notes of the singing Neanderthals" by Jonathan Leake, *The Sunday Times*, 30 January 2005. Reproduced by permission of News Syndication. p.73 Adapted extract from "Discover the joy of reading", *Hendon and Finchley Times*. Reproduced by permission of Newsquest London Ltd. p.74 Adapted extract from "Poles apart from just walking" by Caroline Cook, *Hendon and Finchley Times*. Reproduced by permission of Newsquest London Ltd. p.76 Adapted extract from "Those Brilliant Fall Outfits May Be Saving Trees" by Carl Zimmer from *The New York Times*, 19 October 2004 © 2004 The New York Times. All rights reserved. Used by permission and protected by the Copyright Laws of the United States. The printing, copying, redistribution, or transmission of this Content without express written permission is prohibited. p.80 Adapted extract from "Major Tim Peake: how I became a British astronaut" by Tim Peake, *The Telegraph*, 5 January 2014 © Telegraph Media Group Limited 2014. Reproduced by permission. p.83 Adapted extract from "Roland Paoletti – Obituary", *The Telegraph*, 19 November 2013 © Telegraph Media Group Limited 2013. Reproduced by permission. p.86 Adapted extract from "TMG's interview with Jimmy Carr and Lucy Greeves" by Neil Drabble, *The Telegraph*, 29 October 2006 © Telegraph Media Group Limited 2006. Reproduced by permission. p.86 Adapted extract from "Ask Esther" by Esther Rantzen, *First News Children's Newspaper*, Issue 28, 10–16 November 2006. Reproduced by permission of First News. p.88 Adapted extract from "Does your chewing gum really lose its flavour" by Heston Blumenthal, *The Telegraph*, 22 October 2005 © Telegraph Media Group Limited 2005. Reproduced by permission.

Tables on pp.102 and 103 reproduced with permission of Cambridge English Language Assessment © 2014

Sources: p.64 *Over 70 Tried and Tested Great Books to Read Aloud* by Jacqueline Wilson.

Although every effort has been made to trace and contact copyright holders before publication, this has not been possible in some cases. We apologize for any apparent infringement of copyright and if notified, the publisher will be pleased to rectify any errors or omissions at the earliest opportunity.

Contents

Introduction

This book contains:

- four complete Practice Tests for the *Cambridge English Advanced* exam (2015)
- access to an extract from a complete online practice test

Exam content

Reading and Use of English (1 hour 30 minutes)

	Text	Question type	Focus
PART 1	1 short text with 8 gaps	4-option multiple-choice; choose the correct word(s) to fill each gap	vocabulary (meaning of single words, completion of phrases, phrasal verbs, etc.) **8 questions; 8 marks**
PART 2	1 short text with 8 gaps	fill each gap with one word	mostly grammar, some vocabulary **8 questions; 8 marks**
PART 3	1 short text with 8 gaps	use the words given to form the correct word for each gap	word formation **8 questions; 8 marks**
PART 4	6 unrelated sentences, each followed by a single word and a gapped sentence	use the word given to complete the gapped sentence so that it means the same as the first sentence	grammar and vocabulary **6 questions; 12 marks** *(1 mark for each part of the answer, max. 2 marks per question)*
PART 5	1 text (article, fiction, non-fiction)	4-option multiple-choice	comprehension of detail, opinion, attitude, tone, purpose, main idea, implication, text organization features, exemplification, reference, comparison **6 questions; 12 marks**
PART 6	4 short texts	matching opinions with the text they appear in	understanding opinions and attitudes; comparing and contrasting opinions and attitudes across texts **4 questions; 8 marks**
PART 7	1 text with 6 paragraphs missing	choice of 7 paragraphs to fill the gaps	understanding of text structure, links between parts of text **6 questions; 12 marks**
PART 8	1 text divided into sections OR several short texts	matching statements / information to section of text or short text they refer to or appear in	location of specific information; comprehension of paraphrasing **10 questions; 10 marks**

Writing (1 hour 30 minutes)

	Task	Focus
PART 1	essay, based on two points in text given (220–260 words). Candidates **must** do this task.	explaining which of the two points is more important and giving reasons for this opinion **20 marks**
PART 2	letter / email, proposal, report or review (220–260 words) Candidates choose ONE task from three choices.	varies according to the task, including comparing, giving advice, giving opinions, justifying, persuading **20 marks**

Listening (40 minutes)

In the exam, each recording is heard twice. On the CD, they are not repeated, so you will need to play each track again. At the end of the exam, candidates are given 5 minutes to transfer their answers to the answer sheet.

	Recording	Question type	Focus
PART 1	3 short conversations	3-option multiple-choice (2 questions per conversation)	detail, gist, opinion, speaker feeling, attitude, function, purpose, agreement between speakers, course of action **6 questions; 6 marks**
PART 2	1 monologue	sentence completion: 8 sentences to complete with a word or short phrase	understanding of specific information and stated opinion **8 questions; 8 marks**
PART 3	1 interview or conversation (two or more speakers)	4-option multiple-choice	understanding of opinion, attitude, detail, gist, speaker feeling, purpose, function and agreement between speakers **6 questions; 6 marks**
PART 4	5 short monologues	matching: 2 tasks. For each task, match what each speaker says to 1 of 8 options (5 questions per task)	same as Part 1 **10 questions; 10 marks**

Speaking (15 minutes)

	Activity type (examiner + two candidates)	Focus
PART 1	conversation between candidates and interlocutor (2 mins)	general and personal topics relating to the candidate
PART 2	individual 'long turn' for each candidate with a brief response from second candidate (4 mins) candidates talk about 2 sets of 3 pictures	organizing a larger unit of discourse, comparing, describing, expressing opinions and speculating
PART 3	2-way conversation between candidates (4 mins) candidates discuss written prompts in a decision-making task	interaction, exchanging ideas, expressing and justifying opinions, agreeing and / or disagreeing, suggesting, speculating, evaluating, reaching a decision through negotiation
PART 4	conversation between candidates and interlocutor (5 mins) candidates discuss topics related to Part 3 task with the examiner	expressing and justifying opinions, agreeing and / or disagreeing, speculating **40 marks total**

The Reading and Use of English paper carries 40% of the total. The Writing, Listening and Speaking papers each carry 20% of the total.

Reading and Use of English (1 hour 30 minutes)

PART 1

For questions 1–8, read the text below and decide which answer (A, B, C or D) best fits each gap. There is an example at the beginning (0).

Mark your answers on the separate answer sheet.

Example:

0 **A** interfering   **B** upsetting   **C** damaging   **D** intruding

0	A	B	C	D

Taking photographs ruins the memory, research finds

Our obsession with recording every detail of our happiest moments could be **0**_____ our ability to remember them, according to new research.

Dr Linda Henkel, from Fairfield University, Connecticut, described this as the 'photo-taking impairment effect'. She said, 'People often whip out their cameras almost mindlessly to **1**_____ a moment, to the point that they are missing what is happening **2**_____ in front of them. When people rely on technology to remember for them – **3**_____ on the camera to record the event and thus not needing to **4**_____ to it fully themselves – it can have a negative **5**_____ on how well they remember their experiences.'

In Dr Henkel's experiment, a group of university students were **6**_____ on a tour of a museum and asked to either photograph or try to remember objects on display. The next day each student's memory was tested. The results showed that people were less **7**_____ in recognizing the objects they had photographed **8**_____ with those they had only looked at.

1	**A** seize	**B** grasp	**C** capture	**D** snatch
2	**A** quite	**B** right	**C** merely	**D** barely
3	**A** counting	**B** settling	**C** assuming	**D** swearing
4	**A** engage	**B** apply	**C** attend	**D** dedicate
5	**A** result	**B** aspect	**C** extent	**D** impact
6	**A** steered	**B** run	**C** led	**D** conveyed
7	**A** accurate	**B** faithful	**C** exact	**D** factual
8	**A** measured	**B** compared	**C** matched	**D** confronted

For questions **9–16**, read the text below and think of the word which best fits each gap. Use only **one** word in each gap. There is an example at the beginning (**0**).

Write your answers **IN CAPITAL LETTERS** on the separate answer sheet.

Example:

0	T	O														

On the hunt for the best young female entrepreneurs

Founded in 1972, the Veuve Clicquot Business Woman Award is celebrated in 27 countries. Veuve Clicquot has now introduced a new award **0** _____ complement its Business Woman of the Year category. Called The New Generation Award, **9** _____ recognizes the best young female talent across business and corporate life.

The first winner of the award, Kathryn Parsons, **10** _____ innovative start-up company, Decoded, teaches people to code in a day, has joined the judging panel to help find this year's winner. 'The importance of these awards cannot **11** _____ overestimated,' she says. 'Women need role models that prove to **12** _____ that they can do it, too.'

The New Generation Award is open to entrepreneurial businesswomen **13** _____ the ages of 25 and 35. They can run **14** _____ own businesses or hail from corporate life. 'This award isn't about how much money you've made or how long you've been in business, it's about recognizing young women **15** _____ a mission and a vision,' says Parsons. 'We want to meet women who are working to **16** _____ the world a better place.'

PART 3

For questions 17–24, read the text below. Use the word given in capitals at the end of some of the lines to form a word that fits in the gap in the same line. There is an example at the beginning (0).

Write your answers IN CAPITAL LETTERS on the separate answer sheet.

Example:

| 0 | R | E | S | I | G | N | A | T | I | O | N | | | | | | | |

EXIT INTERVIEWS

If you are thinking of leaving your job, you may think that handing

in your letter of **0**_____ is the end of the matter. But an increasing   RESIGN

number of companies now conduct 'exit interviews' with staff.

   For the employee, an exit interview may feel like an ideal opportunity

to rant and rave about every little **17**_____ that has troubled them   ANNOY

since they got the job. But, **18**_____ in mind that you will probably   BEAR

still need a **19**_____ from these people, it is best to avoid getting   REFER

angry or **20**_____ , and just answer the questions as calmly and   EMOTION

with as much **21**_____ as possible.   HONEST

   For employers, the exit interview is a rare opportunity to gather some

valuable information about the way staff perceive the company.

Existing employees may not wish to cause **22**_____ to the boss or   OFFEND

damage their chances of promotion, so are unlikely to **23**_____   CLOSE

their real feelings about the company. However, someone who has already

resigned is more likely to be **24**_____ when giving their opinions.   TRUE

PART 4

For questions 25–30, complete the second sentence so that it has a similar meaning to the first sentence, using the word given. **Do not change the word given.** *You must use between* **three** *and* **six** *words, including the word given. Here is an example (*0*).*

Example:

0 I didn't know the way there, so I got lost.

GET

Not _____ there, I got lost.

0	K N O W I N G H O W T O G E T

Write **only** *the missing words* **IN CAPITAL LETTERS** *on the separate answer sheet.*

---

25 I've just noticed that the car has almost run out of petrol.

HARDLY

I've just noticed that _____ left in the car.

26 I didn't know that cars were so expensive in this country.

IDEA

I _____ so much in this country.

27 Don't get depressed because of such a small problem.

LET

It's such a small problem that you shouldn't _____ down.

28 It is reported that he is now recovering in hospital.

RECOVERY

He is reported _____ in hospital now.

29 Laura's teacher says that she doesn't have a serious enough attitude to her work.

SERIOUSLY

Laura doesn't _____ to her teacher.

30 What's confusing you so much?

LOT

What is it that's _____ confusion?

PART 5

You are going to read a book review. For questions 31–36, choose the answer (A, B, C or D) which you think fits best according to the text.

Mark your answers on the separate answer sheet.

The Great Indoors: At Home in the Modern British House
by Ben Highmore

In 1910 the music hall comedian Billy Williams scored his biggest hit with the song *When Father Papered the Parlour*, mocking the incompetence of the amateur home decorator. Fifty years later, comedians Norman Wisdom and Bruce Forsyth were still entertaining millions on the TV show *Sunday Night at the London Palladium* with a similar routine, but the joke was starting to look dated. The success of magazines such as *The Practical Householder* was already proving that, as the 1957 Ideal Home Exhibition proclaimed, 'Do-it-yourself is a home hobby that is here to stay.'

By this stage, Britain had mostly completed its transition from primitive housing conditions, made bearable – for those who could afford it – by servants and handymen, into a world where families looked after themselves in highly serviced environments. Recognisably modern technology, in the form of telephones, televisions and electricity, had become ubiquitous and was to transform domestic living still further in the coming years. The makeover of British homes in the twentieth century is recounted in Ben Highmore's entertaining and informative new book. He takes us on a whirlwind tour of an everyday house, from entrance hall to garden shed, illuminated by extensive reference to oral histories, popular magazines and personal memoirs.

At its centre, though, is the way that our homes have reflected wider social changes. There is the decline of formality, so that living rooms once full of heavy furniture and Victorian knick-knacks are now dominated by television screens and littered with children's toys. There is a growing internationalism in taste. And there is the rise of domestic democracy, with the household radiogram and telephone (located in the hall) now replaced by iPads, laptops and mobiles in virtually every room. Key to that decentralization of the home – and the implied shift of power within it – is the advent of central heating, which gets pride of place as the innovation that allowed the whole house to become accessible at all times of day and night. Telling an unruly child to 'go to your room' no longer seems much of a threat.

Highmore also documents, however, some less successful steps in the onward march of domestic machinery. Whatever happened to the gas-powered fridges we were promised in 1946? Or to the Dishmaster a decade later that promised to do 'a whole day's washing up in just three minutes'? Rather more clear is the reason why a 1902 Teasmade failed to catch on: 'when the alarm clock triggered the switch, a match was struck, lighting a spirit stove under the kettle'. You don't have to be a health and safety fanatic to conclude that a bedroom isn't the ideal place for such a gadget.

Equally disturbing to the modern reader is the pre-war obsession with children getting fresh air. It was a belief so entrenched that even a voice of dissent merely argued that in winter, 'The healthy child only needs about three hours a day in the open air, as long as the day and night nursery windows are always open.' Nowadays, the fresh air obsession has been replaced by irrational fears of horrors outside the home. It's easier to laugh at the foibles of the past, and Highmore doesn't always resist a sense of modern superiority, though, for the most part, he's an engaging and quirky guide, dispensing sociological insights without jargon.

The message is that even the language of the home has changed irrevocably: airing cupboards are going the same way as drawing rooms. As for that Billy Williams song, 'By the 1980s', Highmore writes, 'it would be impossible for anyone to imagine their front room as a "parlour" without seeming deeply old-fashioned.' He's not entirely correct, for there was at least one person who was still employing such terminology. Prime Minister Margaret Thatcher sold her message with the use of what she called 'the parables of the parlour', which suggests she understood the truth that, despite the catalogue of changes, there is a core that seems consistent. A 1946 edition of *Housewife* magazine spelt it out: 'men make houses, women make homes'. When you watch a male comedian today doing a routine about his wife's attachment to scatter cushions, it seems worth asking: has the family dynamic really moved a great deal?'

31 The reviewer's main topic in the first paragraph is

  A improvements in home decorating skills.
  B how common it was for home decorating to be discussed.
  C how unfair descriptions of home decorating used to be.
  D a change in attitudes to home decorating.

31

32 In the second paragraph, the reviewer says that the book includes evidence illustrating

  A that some British people's homes were transformed more than others.
  B the widespread nature of changes that took place in British homes.
  C the perceived disadvantages of certain developments in British homes.
  D that the roles of certain people in British homes changed enormously.

32

33 In the third paragraph, the reviewer points to a change in

  A the extent to which different parts of the house are occupied.
  B ideas of which parts of a house should be furnished in a formal way.
  C how much time children spend in their own rooms.
  D beliefs about what the most pleasant aspect of home life is.

33

34 The reviewer suggests in the fourth paragraph that

  A most unsuccessful inventions failed because they were dangerous.
  B various unsuccessful inventions failed because they did not work properly.
  C some unsuccessful inventions were not advertised appropriately.
  D there were unsuccessful inventions which might have been good ideas.

34

35 In the fifth paragraph, the reviewer says that in his book, Highmore

  A sometimes focuses on strange ideas that were not very common in the past.
  B occasionally applies the standards of today to practices in the past.
  C occasionally expresses regret about how some attitudes have changed.
  D sometimes includes topics that are not directly relevant to the main topic.

35

36 In the final paragraph, the reviewer suggests that Highmore may be wrong about

  A when certain modern attitudes to home life first developed.
  B which changes in home life in Britain have been most widely welcomed.
  C the extent to which home life in Britain has changed.
  D how common terms such as 'airing cupboards' are in modern Britain.

36

You are going to read four reviews of a documentary series on TV about large companies. For questions 37–40, *choose from the reviews* A–D. *The reviews may be chosen more than once.*

Mark your answers *on the separate answer sheet*.

Inside Business

Four reviewers comment on the TV documentary series *Inside Business*, which investigated the workings of a number of large companies

A

The companies that were the focus of each programme in the series *Inside Business* were very diverse in terms of the nature of their business and the way they operated, but between them they demonstrated many of the key features that characterize big organizations in the modern world. Each programme focused mostly on the people at the top. The amount of jargon they used is likely to have been too much for many viewers to contend with, and they may well have given up. If they did stick with the series, however, they will have been left in no doubt as to how complex the business of running large organizations is for those charged with doing so. This was clear from what the interviewees said, but the questioning was not probing enough, and they were not asked to explain or justify the sweeping statements they made.

B

The overwhelming impression given to any viewer who watched all six episodes of *Inside Business* was of the extraordinary pressure that those running modern companies are obliged to operate under. Unless they themselves had experience of working in large companies, however, they are likely to have found some of the interviews bewildering – the questioning was very much of the 'one insider to another' variety and many viewers will have struggled to follow what was being discussed. This aspect detracted somewhat from what was an otherwise compelling insight into the workings of modern companies and may well have caused many viewers to change channels. That's a shame because in general the companies featured in the series illustrated very well the impact of modern management theories on a range of large organizations.

C

You didn't need to know anything about business to be fascinated by the series *Inside Business*, which gave an intriguing picture from the inside of how various household name companies actually operate. The companies chosen made for good television because they all had very individual cultures and ways of operating, and as such could not be said to typify the norm in the world of the modern company. Entertaining as this was, the portrayal of the firms begged all sorts of questions which were not touched on in the interviews. These gave the people in charge a very easy ride indeed, never challenging them to back up their often vague and contentious pronouncements on their approach to leadership. Indeed, the viewer will have been left with the surprising feeling that many large and apparently successful organizations are run by people who enjoy their roles enormously because they avoid the harder aspects of responsibility by delegating them to others.

D

The series *Inside Business* took a serious look at day-to-day life in a modern large company and it wasn't for the casual viewer. The series required some effort to get to grips with the issues covered, in particular in the interviews, which were not really accessible to the lay person and were instead conducted as one expert to another. Having said that, the viewer who did put the effort in was rewarded with an absorbing insight into the workings of these well-known firms. They had each been carefully chosen to be representative of how large companies are structured and function at present, and they had much in common with each other. The main message put across was how adept those in charge have to be in adapting to a constantly changing business world.

Which reviewer

has a different opinion from the others on the choice of companies to focus on in the series? `37`

shares reviewer B's opinion of the likelihood of viewers losing interest in the series after a while? `38`

takes a different view from the others on the impression given in the series of what it is like to be at the top of a large organization? `39`

has a similar view to reviewer C on the questions asked in the interviews in the series? `40`

PART 7

You are going to read a newspaper article about a ship carrying goods across the Atlantic ocean. Six paragraphs have been removed from the article. Choose from the paragraphs A–G the one which fits each gap (41–46). There is one extra paragraph which you do not need to use.

Mark your answers on the separate answer sheet.

The wind-lashed workers who battle the Atlantic in winter

Even at this stormy time of year in Britain, there are thousands of oil workers and fishermen offshore, as well as a scattering of seafarers manning the container ships and tankers that bring us almost everything we need. So it was that in the depths of bitter winter, hoping to learn what modern sailors' lives are like, I joined the Maersk *Pembroke*, a container freighter, on her regular run from Europe to Montreal. She looked so dreadful when I found her in Antwerp that I hoped I had the wrong ship.

41

Trade between Europe and North America is a footnote to the great west–east and north–south runs: companies leave it to older vessels. *Pembroke* is battered and rusty, reeking of diesel and fishy chemicals. She is noisy, her bridge and stairwells patrolled by whistling drafts which rise to howls at sea. Her paintwork is wretched. The Atlantic has stripped her bow back to a rusted steel snarl.

42

It felt like a desperate enterprise on a winter night, as the tide raced us down the Scheldt estuary and

spat us out into the North Sea. According to the weather satellites, the Atlantic was storms from coast to coast, two systems meeting in the middle of our course. On the far side, ice awaited. We were behind schedule, the captain desperate for speed. 'Six-metre waves are OK; any bigger you have to slow down or you kill your ship,' he said. 'Maybe we'll be lucky!'

43

Soon enough, we were in the midst of those feared storms. A nightmare in darkness, a north Atlantic storm is like a wild dream by day, a region of racing elements and livid colour, bursting turquoise foam, violent sunlight, and darkening magenta waves. There is little you can do once committed except lash everything down and enjoy what sleep you can before it becomes impossible. *Pembroke* is more than 200m long and weighs more than 38,000 tons, but the swells threw her about like a tin toy.

44

When they hit us squarely, the whole ship reared, groaning and staggering, shuddered by shocking force. We plunged and tottered for three days before there was a

lull. But even then, an ordinary day involved unpleasant jobs in extreme conditions. I joined a welding party that descended to the hold: a dripping, tilting cathedral composed of vast tanks of toxins and organophosphates, where a rusted hatch cover defied a cheap grinder blade in a fountain of sparks. As we continued west, the wind thickened with sleet, then snow as the next storm arrived.

45

All was well in that regard and, after the storms, we were relieved to enter the St Lawrence River. The ice was not thick enough to hinder us; we passed Quebec City in a glittering blue dawn and made Montreal after sunset, its downtown towers rising out of the tundra night. Huge trucks came for our containers.

46

But without them and their combined defiance of the elements there could be nothing like what we call 'life' at all. Seafarers are not sentimental, but some are quite romantic. They would like to think we thought of them, particularly when the forecast says storms at sea.

A Others felt the same. We were 'the only idiots out here', as several men remarked. We felt our isolation like vulnerability; proof that we had chosen obscure, quixotic lives.

B Going out on deck in such conditions tempted death. Nevertheless, the ship's electrician climbed a ladder out there every four hours to check that the milk, cheese and well-travelled Argentine beef we carried were still frozen in refrigerated containers.

C But it does not take long to develop affection for a ship, even the *Pembroke* — the time it takes her to carry you beyond swimming distance from land, in fact. When I learnt what was waiting for us mid-ocean I became her ardent fan, despite all those deficiencies.

D There were Dutch bulbs, seaweed fertilizer from Tanzania, Iranian dates for Colombia, Sri Lankan tea bags, Polish glue, Hungarian tyres, Indian seeds, and much besides. The sailors are not told what they carry. They just keep the ships going.

E Hoping so, we slipped down-Channel in darkness, with the Dover coastguard wishing us, 'Good watch, and a safe passage to your destination.' The following evening we left the light of Bishop Rock on the Scilly Isles behind. 'When we see that again we know we're home,' said the second mate.

F Huge black monsters marched at us out of the north west, striped with white streaks of foam running out of the wind's mouth. The ocean moved in all directions at once and the waves became enormous, charging giants of liquid emerald, each demanding its own reckoning.

G That feeling must have been obvious to the captain. 'She's been all over the world,' proud Captain Koop, a grey-bristled Dutchman, as quick and confident as a Master Mariner must be, told me. 'She was designed for the South Pacific,' he said, wistfully.

PART 8

You are going to read an article about some children. For questions 47–56, choose from the sections of the article (A–E). The sections may be chosen more than once. When more than one answer is required, these may be given in any order.

Mark your answers on the separate answer sheet.

In which section of the article are the following mentioned?

an example of a sign that has become simpler	47
the difference between how the deaf children communicate an image and how other people communicate the same image	48
the fact that the same signs can be used in the communication of a number of ideas	49
the characteristics of languages in general at different stages of their development	50
a belief that language is learnt by means of a specific part of the mind	51
an aspect of language learning that children are particularly good at	52
how regularly the children have been monitored	53
older children passing their sign language on to younger children	54
the reason why the children created a particular sign	55
opposing views on how people acquire language	56

DEAF CHILDREN'S AD HOC LANGUAGE EVOLVES AND INSTRUCTS

A A deep insight into the way the brain learns language has emerged from the study of Nicaraguan sign language, invented by deaf children in a Nicaraguan school as a means of communicating among themselves. The Nicaraguan children are well-known to linguists because they provide an apparently unique example of people inventing a language from scratch. The phenomenon started at a school for special education founded in 1977. Instructors noticed that the deaf children, while absorbing little from their Spanish lessons, had developed a system of signs for talking to one another. As one generation of children taught the system to the next, it evolved from a set of gestures into a far more sophisticated form of communication, and today's 800 users of the language provide a living history of the stages of formation.

B The children have been studied principally by Dr. Judy Kegi, a linguist at the University of Southern Maine, and Dr. Ann Senghas, a cognitive scientist at Columbia University in New York City. In the latest study, published in *Science* magazine, Dr. Senghas shows that the younger children have now decomposed certain gestures into smaller component signs. A hearing person asked to mime a standard story about a cat waddling down a street will make a single gesture, a downward spiral motion of the hand. But the deaf children have developed two different signs to use in its place.

They sign a circle for the rolling motion and then a straight line for the direction of movement. This requires more signing, but the two signs can be used in combination with others to express different concepts. The development is of interest to linguists because it captures a principal quality of human language – discrete elements usable in different combinations – in contrast to the one sound, one meaning of animal communication. 'The regularity she documents here – mapping discrete aspects of the world onto discrete word choices – is one of the most distinctive properties of human language,' said Dr. Steven Pinker, a cognitive scientist at Harvard University.

C When people with no common language are thrown into contact, they often develop an ad hoc language known to linguists as a pidgin language, usually derived from one of the parent languages. Pidgins are rudimentary systems with minimal grammar and utterances. But in a generation or two, the pidgins acquire grammar and become upgraded to what linguists call creoles. Though many new languages have been created by the pidgin-creole route, the Nicaraguan situation is unique, Dr. Senghas said, because its starting

point was not a complex language but ordinary gestures. From this raw material, the deaf children appear to be spontaneously fabricating the elements of language.

D Linguists have been engaged in a longstanding argument as to whether there is an innate, specialized neural machinery for learning language, as proposed by Noam Chomsky of the Massachusetts Institute of Technology, or whether everything is learned from scratch. Dr. Senghas says her finding supports the view that language learning is innate, not purely cultural, since the Nicaraguan children's disaggregation of gestures appears to be spontaneous. Her result also upholds the idea that children play an important part in converting a pidgin into a creole. Because children's minds are primed to learn the rules of grammar, it is thought, they spontaneously impose grammatical structure on a pidgin that doesn't have one.

E The Nicaraguan children are a living laboratory of language generation. Dr. Senghas, who has been visiting their school every year since 1990, said she had noticed how the signs for numbers have developed. Originally the children represented '20' by

flicking the fingers of both hands in the air twice. But this cumbersome sign has been replaced with a form that can now be signed with one hand. The children don't care that the new sign doesn't look like a 20, Dr. Senghas said; they just want a symbol that can be signed fast.

Writing (1 hour 30 minutes)

PART 1

You must answer this question. Write your answer in 220–260 words in an appropriate style.

---

1   Your class has attended a panel discussion on the subject of TV shows that feature members of the public, such as reality TV shows and talent competitions. You have made the notes below.

> Aspects of reality and talent TV shows
>
> • entertainment for viewers
>
> • influence on young people
>
> • effect on participants

> Some opinions expressed in the discussion:
>
> 'These programmes are just harmless entertainment and there is nothing wrong with them.'
>
> 'The influence these programmes can have on young people can be very bad indeed.'
>
> 'People who take part in these programmes can be damaged by the experience.'

Write an **essay** for your tutor discussing **two** of the aspects in your notes. You should **explain which aspect you think is the most important** regarding these TV shows and **provide reasons** to support your opinion.

You may, if you wish, make use of the opinions expressed in the discussion, but you should use your own words as far as possible.

PART 2

Write an answer to one of the questions 2–4 in this part. Write your answer in 220–260 words in an appropriate style.

2   You see the following announcement in an international magazine.

PRODUCT REVIEWS WANTED

Have you bought a new product recently, or had one bought for you? Maybe you've just got a new gadget or piece of technology or equipment. It could be something for work or leisure. We'd like to hear what you think of it for our Readers' Reviews Page. Describe the product for readers and give your opinions on it. Do you recommend it? If so, why? If not, why not? Send your review to the address below.

Write your review.

3   You see the following notice in the place where you work or study.

ANNIVERSARY EVENT PROPOSALS

As you may know, next year we will have been in existence for 20 years, and at a recent meeting it was decided that we should hold a special event to celebrate this achievement. We're now looking for proposals as to what kind of event to hold. Have you got a good idea for a special event to celebrate our 20th anniversary? Put together a proposal, giving details of your idea and how the event could be organized. We'll consider all the proposals at a meeting next month.

Write your proposal.

4   Your company is going to make a video for publicity reasons, showing what the company does and the people who work there. Your manager has asked you to write a letter to all members of staff telling them about plans for this video. Your letter should explain:

■   why the video is going to be made
■   what the video will contain
■   what staff members will be asked to do.

Write your letter.

Listening (40 minutes)

PART 1

You will hear three different extracts. For questions 1–6, choose the answer (A, B or C) which fits best according to what you hear. There are two questions for each extract.

Extract One
You hear two people talking about public speaking.

1   Both speakers refer to a feeling of

   A   over-confidence.
   B   embarrassment.
   C   achievement.

   [ ] 1

2   The two speakers agree that a big problem with speaking in public is

   A   losing the audience's attention during a speech.
   B   choosing the wrong content for a speech.
   C   feeling nervous at the thought of giving a speech.

   [ ] 2

Extract Two
You hear part of a radio programme about the London Underground.

3   The poster campaign came at a time when

   A   various aspects of life in London were changing.
   B   many people were reluctant to travel on the Underground.
   C   the use of posters for advertising was increasing.

   [ ] 3

4   What does Zoe say about the content of the posters?

   A   It only appealed to a certain type of person.
   B   It contrasted with real life for many people.
   C   It influenced the lifestyles of some people.

   [ ] 4

Extract Three
You hear two people discussing the news media.

5   What opinion does the man express about the news media?

   A   It doesn't deserve its reputation.
   B   It has become more influential.
   C   Its standards have risen.

   [ ] 5

6   The woman mentions medical stories

   A   to explain her attitude to the news media.
   B   to illustrate the importance of the news media.
   C   to describe why people dislike the news media.

   [ ] 6

PART 2

You will hear part of a talk about the invention of the microwave oven.
For questions 7–14, complete the sentences with a word or short phrase.

THE INVENTION OF THE MICROWAVE OVEN

The invention of the microwave oven began when a chocolate peanut bar

[_____ 7] in Percy Spencer's pocket.

Spencer had previously invented a method for [_____ 8] the tubes
used in radar equipment.

Spencer's first experiment involved putting [_____ 9] near to some
radar equipment.

In his next experiment, an egg was put into a kettle and it [_____ 10].

The first microwave oven was set up in [_____ 11] in Boston in 1946.

The first microwave oven got its name as a result of [_____ 12] at
the company.

One problem with the first microwave oven was that [_____ 13] did
not change colour in it.

When a microwave oven that could be placed on top of a [_____ 14]
was produced, sales began to rise.

You will hear a radio interview with someone who has been having ballet lessons. For questions 15–20, choose the answer (A, B, C or D) which fits best according to what you hear.

15 What does Rupert say about the fact that he is doing ballet classes?

A Other people have ridiculed him for it.
B He expects to be mocked for it.
C It is not as unusual as people might think.
D People may think it isn't really true.

15 ☐

16 Rupert says that before he started doing ballet lessons

A he had been doing routine physical fitness training.
B his knowledge of ballet had been growing.
C ballet had taken over from football as his greatest interest.
D he had been considering doing ballroom dancing again.

16 ☐

17 Rupert says that when the idea of ballet lessons was suggested to him,

A he thought it was a joke.
B he was unsure exactly what would be involved.
C he began to have unrealistic expectations of what he could achieve.
D he initially lacked the confidence to do it.

17 ☐

18 One of the advantages of ballet that Rupert mentions is that

A it leads to fewer injuries than other physical activities.
B it has both physical and mental effects.
C it is particularly good for certain parts of the body.
D it is more interesting than other forms of exercise.

18 ☐

19 What does Rupert say about the sessions?

A The content of them is varied.
B Some of the movements in them are harder than others for him.
C All of the movements in them have to be done accurately.
D They don't all involve basic movements.

19 ☐

20 What does Rupert say about his progress at ballet?

A It has been much more rapid than he had expected.
B It has made him consider giving up his other training.
C It has given him greater appreciation of the skills of professionals.
D It has led him to enrol for certain exams.

20 ☐

PART 4

You will hear five short extracts in which people are talking about people they know.

Task one

For questions 21–25, choose from the list A–H the description each speaker gives of the person.

A critical

B easily influenced

C tough

D careless

E moody

F cruel

G arrogant

H deceitful

Speaker 1 ☐ **21**

Speaker 2 ☐ **22**

Speaker 3 ☐ **23**

Speaker 4 ☐ **24**

Speaker 5 ☐ **25**

Task two

For questions 26–30, choose from the list A–H the feeling each speaker expresses about the person.

A sympathy

B confusion

C loyalty

D amusement

E guilt

F envy

G fear

H annoyance

Speaker 1 ☐ **26**

Speaker 2 ☐ **27**

Speaker 3 ☐ **28**

Speaker 4 ☐ **29**

Speaker 5 ☐ **30**

While you listen you must complete both tasks.

Speaking (15 minutes)

PART 1 (2 minutes)

- Where do you come from?
- What's your job / What are you studying?
- How long have you been learning English?
- What do you like most and least about your job / course? ..... (Why?)

- How does a typical day for you start?
- Would you say that you have an exciting social life? ..... (Why? / Why not?)
- What kind of books do you like most? ..... (Why?)
- Do you try to keep fit? If so, how? If not, why not?
- Describe the people that you work / study with.
- What hobby / hobbies do you have?
- What are your aims and ambitions for the future?
- What kind of things cause you stress?

PART 2 (4 minutes)

1 **Characters on TV**
2 **Things that annoy people**

Candidate A	Look at the three photographs 1A, 1B and 1C on page 25 They show **scenes from different TV series.**
	Compare two of the photographs and say **what each series might be about, and what the characters might be like.**
	Candidate A talks on his / her own for 1 minute.
Candidate B	**Which of the series would you prefer to watch, and why?**
	Candidate B talks on his / her own for about 30 seconds.
Candidate B	Look at the three photographs 2A, 2B and 2C on page 25. They show **things that often annoy people.**
	Compare two of the photographs and say **why people find these things annoying, and what can be done about them.**
	Candidate B talks on his / her own for 1 minute.
Candidate A	**Which of these things annoys you the most, and why?**
	Candidate A talks on his / her own for about 30 seconds.

PART 2

- What might each TV series be about?
- What might the characters be like?

1A

1B

1C

- Why do these things annoy people?
- What can be done about them?

2A

2B

2C

PART 3 (4 minutes) and PART 4 (5 minutes)

Tourism

PART 3

Look at page 27, where there are some things that tourists might do before or during a trip to another country.

First, talk to each other **about how important it is for tourists to do these things before or during a trip to another country.**

Candidates A and B discuss this together for about 2 minutes.

Now decide **which of these things is the most important for tourists to do.**

Candidates A and B discuss this together for about 1 minute.

PART 4

- What changes have taken place in tourism in recent times?
- Some people say that tourism does more harm than good. Do you agree?
- Which people benefit the most and the least from modern tourism?
- What is the difference between 'tourists' and 'travellers'? Do you think it is better to be one than the other? (Why? / Why not?)
- Some people say that because of tourism, countries all over the world are becoming more similar to each other? Do you agree? Is this a desirable development?
- What developments do you think there will be in tourism in the future?

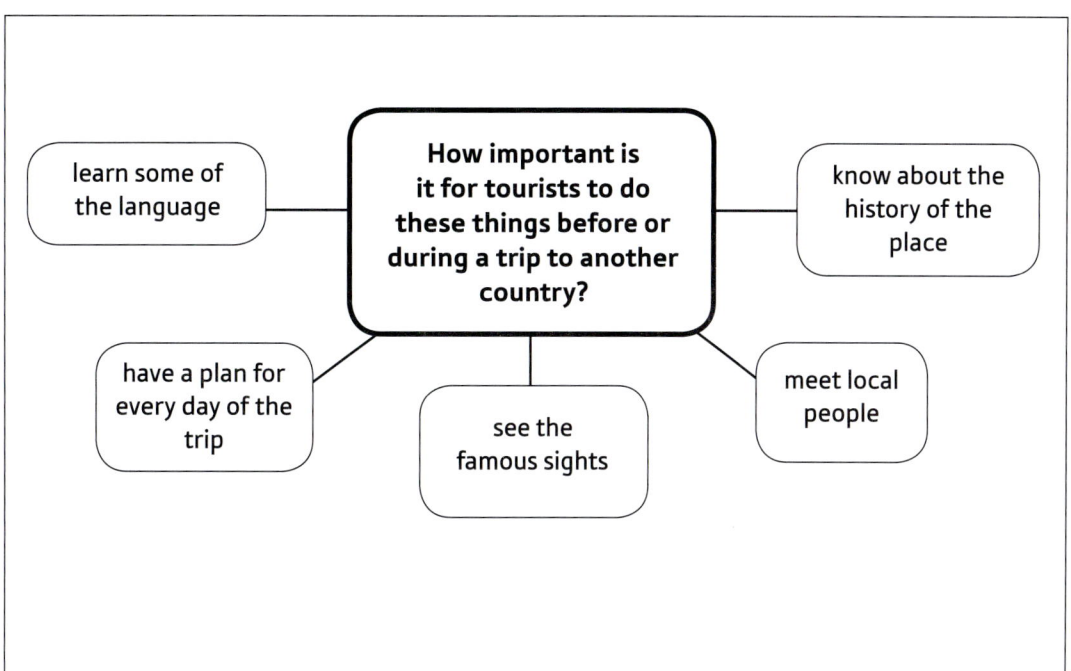

Reading and Use of English (1 hour 30 minutes)

PART 1

For questions 1–8, read the text below and decide which answer (A, B, C or D) best fits each gap. There is an example at the beginning (0).

Mark your answers on the separate answer sheet.

Example:

0 **A** original **B** initial **C** primary **D** novel

0	**A**	**B**	**C**	**D**

Mary Heath, female pilot

Mary Heath was the **0**_____ Queen of the Skies, one of the best-known women in the world during the **1**_____ age of aviation. She was the first woman in Britain to gain a commercial pilot's licence, the first to **2**_____ a parachute jump – and the first British women's javelin champion. She scandalized 1920s' British society by marrying three times (at the **3**_____ of her fame she wed politician Sir James Heath – her second husband, 45 years her senior).

In 1928, aged 31, she became the first pilot to fly an open-cockpit plane, solo, from South Africa to Egypt, **4**_____ 9,000 miles in three months. It was a triumph. Lady Heath was **5**_____ as the nation's sweetheart and called 'Lady Icarus' by the press. However, her life was **6**_____ tragically short. Only a year later, she **7**_____ a horrific accident at the National Air Show in Ohio in the USA, when her plane crashed through the roof of a building. Her health was never the **8**_____ again, and she died in May 1939.

1	**A** golden	**B** sweet	**C** bright	**D** shiny
2	**A** put	**B** hold	**C** take	**D** make
3	**A** crest	**B** height	**C** fullness	**D** top
4	**A** covering	**B** stretching	**C** crossing	**D** ranging
5	**A** exclaimed	**B** declared	**C** hailed	**D** quoted
6	**A** cut	**B** left	**C** stopped	**D** brought
7	**A** undertook	**B** suffered	**C** received	**D** underwent
8	**A** like	**B** equal	**C** better	**D** same

For questions **9–16**, read the text below and think of the word which best fits each gap. Use only **one** word in each gap. There is an example at the beginning (**0**).

Write your answers **IN CAPITAL LETTERS** *on the separate answer sheet*.

Example:

0	A	S													

TRIATHLETES

Stuart Hayes had launched himself on a promising career **0**_____ a swimmer when something odd happened **9**_____ him at the local pool. Flogging up and down for the umpteenth time, he suddenly realized **10**_____ bored he had become with the monotony. Wasn't there a more interesting way of **11**_____ sporty, for heaven's sake? There was and there is: the colour, sweat and sheer emotion of triathlons. Stuart became a world-class triathlete and won the London Triathlon, the biggest event of **12**_____ kind in the world.

Triathlons are **13**_____ but boring. Combining swimming, cycling and running in one physical onslaught, they offer huge variety within a single racing framework. In Britain, the sport is growing by 10 per cent a year. 'People are moving away **14**_____ just running, and are looking for new challenges,' says Nick Rusling, event director for the London Triathlon. 'Triathlons are a **15**_____ deal more interesting to train for and you can vary training to fit busy lifestyles, swimming in your lunch break and **16**_____ on.

For questions 17–24, read the text below. Use the word given in capitals at the end of some of the lines to form a word that fits in the gap in the same line. There is an example at the beginning (0).

Write your answers IN CAPITAL LETTERS *on the separate answer sheet.*

Example:

| 0 | W | I | N | N | E | R | | | | | | | |

RESTAURANT OF THE YEAR

One more chance! That's all we're giving you to tell us about your

favourite restaurant and boost its chances of becoming the **0**_____   WIN

of our Restaurant of the Year competition. This is the last time the

official **17**_____ form will appear in the paper and next Thursday   NOMINATE

is the final date for **18**_____ of completed forms.   RECEIVE

     Over the past few weeks we have been swamped by a paper mountain

as **19**_____ across the city jot down the compelling reasons why   DINE

they believe their **20**_____ restaurant should definitely win our   CHOOSE

hotly **21**_____ competition.   CONTEST

     Once the **22**_____ has passed, our judges will sit down and count   DEAD

all the forms. The three restaurants which receive the most votes will

then be visited by the judges. These visits will of course be

23_____ , so the restaurants themselves will not know that the   ANNOUNCE

judges are there. After their visits, the judges will make their final

decision over who wins the **24**_____ title 'Restaurant of the Year'.   PRESTIGE

PART 4

*For questions 25–30, complete the second sentence so that it has a similar meaning to the first sentence, using the word given. **Do not change the word given.** You must use between* **three** *and* **six** *words, including the word given. Here is an example (**0**).*

Example:

0   I didn't know the way there, so I got lost.

GET

Not _____ there, I got lost.

0	K N O W I N G H O W T O G E T

Write only *the missing words* **IN CAPITAL LETTERS** *on the separate answer sheet.*

---

25   It took me some time to understand fully what happened.

WHILE

It was _____ understood what had happened.

26   There's no point arguing about this small detail, in my opinion.

WORTH

This small detail _____ , in my opinion.

27   If your order is delayed, we will contact you.

DELAY

Should _____ to your order, we will contact you.

28   The two situations are completely different.

COMMON

The two situations don't _____ each other.

29   I was amazed because there were no problems throughout the holiday.

WENT

To _____ wrong throughout the holiday.

30   I have no intention of doing another kind of job.

DREAM

I _____ other kind of job.

PART 5

You are going to read a newspaper article about management. For questions 31–36, choose the answer (A, B, C or D) which you think fits best according to the text.

Mark your answers on the separate answer sheet.

Simply ticking the boxes isn't enough

I have been asked what I think about the idea of 'Investing in People'. The best answer I can give is that I think that what it tries to achieve – basically making the link between business improvement and focusing on the needs of the people who work for an organization – is great. My problem is with organizations who subscribe to it as a way to help them 'get better', when they don't bother to understand where they went wrong in the first place. They need to ask what explicit and implicit policies and procedures they have in place that prevent their people from being able to do the right thing for the right reasons.

I am sure that there are managers out there who don't know any better, and assume that to manage they simply need to put pressure on their people to perform. But people don't demonstrate high performance because they are told to. They do it because they see the need to do it, and make the choice to do so. They do it because they are connected to the business goals and they see how their contributions can help achieve them. Such managers may tell themselves they can put a 'tick' in the 'we care about people' box. But simply putting ticks in boxes is no good if it doesn't reflect reality.

I know of a company that was so concerned that its people were doing the 'right thing' that it put in place a series of metrics to measure their effectiveness. So far, so good. But one of the objectives – making successful sales calls – manifested itself in the

metric 'Number of potential customers seen in one day'. The sales people obviously focused their efforts on going from one customer's office to another, and not on closing deals. Instead of the employees becoming more effective, they focused on getting the boxes ticked. Good intent; poor thinking.

Another company wanted to improve the speed with which it was able to introduce new products. Competition was beating it to the market place, and consequently the company was losing market share. Senior management sent out the message to reduce the time spent in getting products into customers' hands, with the explanation that they couldn't afford delays. This was a relatively easy task, especially since the time spent testing the products was cut in half to accomplish the time reduction. The result was new products were introduced in less time than those of the competition – but soon rejected by customers for poor quality. Good intent; reckless implementation.

A third company I know is trying hard to help employees see that they have some control over their future. The company instituted a programme

with a title like 'Creating our own future' or something like that. A good idea; get the people involved in the future of the company. But instead of the employees becoming motivated to contribute, they saw it as a hollow exercise on the part of senior management who, in the past, had paid little attention to anything other than getting the job done so they could report great earnings. Yes, the programme was a big 'tick the box' effort, but that was all it was in the minds of the people that it was designed for.

A final example is of a company that brought in one of these 'Investing in People' programmes to change the way the company was run. Assessors were running around like crazy, helping managers examine how they managed. They told managers how they could manage better. And when the programme was over, the company was able to say they had done it – it had invested in its people and life was now good. But the managers simply went back to business as usual. After all, the assessors were gone, and they had targets to hit.

All these examples are representative of senior management who see the need to improve things in their organization, but don't see how to do it. For a start, a programme targeted at improving things is only as good as management's ability to motivate their people. And when the employees simply see the programme as a box-ticking exercise, then it's hopeless.

31 The writer thinks that putting the concept of 'Investing in People' into practice

    A frequently results in confusion among the people it is supposed to help.

    B involves more effort than some organizations are prepared to make.

    C may create problems where previously there had not been any problems.

    D is something that some organizations should not attempt to do.

31

32 The writer's main point in the second paragraph is that the performance of employees

    A may be very good even if management is poor.

    B cannot be accurately measured by any box-ticking exercise.

    C is related to their knowledge of the organization as a whole.

    D is not as unpredictable as some managers believe it to be.

32

33 What point does the writer make about the first company he describes?

    A It was not really interested in measuring the effectiveness of employees.

    B The targets that it set for staff were unrealistic.

    C It failed to understand the real needs of its employees.

    D The data that it collected did not measure what it was supposed to measure.

33

34 What point does the writer make about the second company he describes?

    A It made what should have been an easy task into a complicated one.

    B It failed to foresee the consequences of an instruction.

    C It misunderstood why a new approach was required.

    D It refused to take into account the views of employees.

34

35 What does the writer say about the programme introduced by the third company he mentions?

    A Employees did not believe that it had been introduced for their benefit.

    B Employees felt that it was in fact a way of making their jobs even harder.

    C The reason given for introducing it was not the real reason why it was introduced.

    D It was an inappropriate kind of programme for this particular organization.

35

36 The writer says that the programme in his final example

    A was too demanding for managers to maintain long-term.

    B was treated as a self-contained exercise by managers.

    C involved some strange ideas on how managers could improve.

    D caused managers to believe that their previous methods had been better.

36

TEST 2

You are going to read four extracts from introductions to books on popular culture. For questions 37–40, choose from the extracts A–D. The extracts may be chosen more than once.

Mark your answers on the separate answer sheet.

An introduction to popular culture

Four writers summarize their beliefs about various aspects of popular culture

A

The whole concept of 'popular culture' is a relatively modern one and as a phenomenon it is key to the understanding of any modern society. Earnest studies abound on the subject and indeed there are whole branches of academia dedicated to research and theories on the topic, but in many cases what these do is over-complicate something that is in reality a relatively simple matter. Popular culture springs from small groups of like-minded people getting together with new ideas and then it spreads out to the population at large if they find these ideas appealing. Much of it relates to the young and for them it gives a happy sense of being separate from other generations and therefore 'special' in some way.

B

Popular culture may once have sprung from the people themselves, and indeed this was the original definition of the term for many experts, but it is naïve to consider that this remains the case. Instead, it has become something imposed on the public from on high, a business commodity that merely pretends to have its roots in the creativity of 'the people' but in fact is simply a money-making enterprise like any other. What people choose to buy and consume in the area of popular culture speaks volumes about their society and is a main indicator of what that society is like. This is especially true in the area of 'youth culture', where the young gain a sense of self and of belonging via shared tastes and possessions. Studies of popular culture tend to focus on the more exciting aspects and to ignore the more mundane, which ironically are often the most interesting.

C

To summarize it briefly, popular culture is developed by the people for the people and when it has become popular enough, commodified for profit by the business world. Studies of popular culture have proliferated over the years, and experts in the field have developed their own vocabulary and criteria for analysing it. These studies often stress the social aspects rather than the commercial ones. For the younger participants in popular culture, these issues are irrelevant, as what they get from it is a sense of identifying with a particular contemporary group, a comforting sense of community. They are disinclined to analyse this themselves. It is worth remembering, however, that at any age, popular culture is often a minority interest – today's media like to give the impression that the vast majority of people are swept up in it whereas this is frequently not the case.

D

If ordinary members of the public were to read most of the worthy studies of popular culture that academics produce, they would find them overblown and ridiculous in taking such everyday and essentially trivial things so seriously. In the media, excitable journalists and experts exaggerate the importance to most people of the current popular culture phenomena, which in reality do not much occupy the minds of most people. The one area where these observations may not hold true, however, is among the young, where popular culture can have undue influence, encouraging them to acquire unrealistic ideas about how they can live their lives and therefore potentially having a damaging effect on their futures. One of the more interesting aspects of popular culture for all ages is its unpredictability – a new phenomenon can suddenly emerge that grips a section of society and that takes the commercial world entirely by surprise, forcing it to react swiftly to keep up and to capitalize on that latest phenomenon.

Which writer

takes a similar view to writer A on studies of popular culture?   **37**

differs from the others on what causes popular culture to arise?   **38**

shares writer B's opinion on the significance of popular culture?   **39**

has a different opinion from the others on the impact of popular culture on young people?   **40**

You are going to read a review of an art exhibition. Six paragraphs have been removed from the article. Choose from the paragraphs A–G the one which fits each gap (41–46). There is one extra paragraph which you do not need to use.

Mark your answers on the separate answer sheet.

An exhibition of works by the artist John Craxton

'A World of Private Mystery: John Craxton RA' at the Fitzwilliam Museum is a small show, but it does full justice to an artist whose career divides into two parts: the years before and during the Second World War, and the work he did afterwards, when for long periods he lived outside England.

It begins with his small-scale landscapes in pen and ink, pastel, gouache and watercolour. His subject is arcadia, but a distinctly English one in which poets and shepherds sleep and dream amid blasted landscapes under darkening skies. Suffused with longing and foreboding, these works reflect the reality of living in a rain-sodden country under constant threat of foreign invasion.

41

Most of the early work is monochrome. In many landscapes, writhing branches and gnarled tree trunks fill our field of vision. Beneath the surface of the self-consciously 'poetic' motifs, the country he shows in these pictures feels claustrophobic and joyless.

42

As this exhibition makes clear, by the age of 25 Craxton's artistic

identity had matured. With his style, subject matter and working method all fully formed, it is hard to imagine how he would have developed had he remained in England after the war.

43

On his first visit to Greece in 1946, Craxton was swept away by the light, colour, landscape, food and people. The dark cloud that hung over the work he did in England lifts and overnight his palette changes to clear blue, green and white.

44

Goats, fish, cats or a frieze of sailors dancing on the edge of the sea: in the Greek paintings beautiful creatures move naturally across bare rocks and blue waters. The compressed joy you find in these pictures doesn't exist elsewhere in British post-

war art. With a few interruptions, Craxton would spend the rest of his life in Crete.

45

But if there is little exploration or discovery in Craxton's later work, you find instead a sense of fullness and completion, a feeling that in accepting his limitations, he remained true to himself. As he once said, 'I can work best in an atmosphere where life is considered more important than art; then I find it's possible to feel a real person – real people, real elements, real windows – real sun above all. In a life of reality, my imagination really works. I feel like an émigré in London and squashed flat.'

46

It's most noticeable in the works on canvas, especially in formal portraits like his 1946 'Girl with a Cock' and it's there too in the faceted geometric planes of Greek landscapes like his panoramic view of Hydra of 1960–61.

Craxton wasn't an artist of the first rank but he was inimitable. This show is just the right scale and it comes with a beautifully illustrated book about his life and work.

A It comes across this way even when he uses strong colour, as in one sunlit landscape in particular, where the yellow is harsh and the red murky. It's as though he's painting something he'd heard about but never actually seen: sunlight.

B It was not only London that oppressed his spirit, I think, but the overwhelming power of the new art being made in Paris by Picasso, Miró and Léger. In assessing Craxton's work, you have to accept his debt to these artists, and particularly Picasso.

C And though he would paint large-scale murals and design stage sets and tapestries, neither his subject matter nor his style changed in any fundamental way during that period. It may sound harsh, but when he decided to live there permanently, he elected to write himself out of the history of art.

D Indeed, I well remember how I'd step into a large gallery, hung floor to ceiling with paintings, and out of the visual cacophony a single picture would leap off the wall. It was always by John Craxton.

E My guess is he'd have responded badly to market forces and critical pressure to do new things. What he needed was to develop at his own pace – even if at times that meant standing still. But to do that he had to leave the country.

F They do so through tightly hatched lines and expressive distortion which ratchet up the emotional intensity, as in his illustrations for an anthology of poetry. In these, a single male figure waits and watches in a dark wood by moonlight.

G Gone are his melancholy self-portraits in the guise of a shepherd or poet – and in their place we find real shepherds (or rather goatherds) tending living animals. Now Craxton is painting a world outside himself, not one that existed largely in his imagination.

You are going to read an article about various birds in Britain. For questions **47–56**, choose from the birds (**A–D**). The birds may be chosen more than once.

Mark your answers **on the separate answer sheet**.

Of which bird are the following stated?

Further attempts to increase its numbers were made once initial attempts had proved successful.

47

Its population growth is a reflection of how tough it is.

48

There is statistical evidence to support the view that it is a very popular bird.

49

There was a particular period when its population plummeted.

50

A criticism could be made of its physical appearance.

51

A common perception of it has proved inaccurate.

52

Growth in its numbers has been much more gradual than desired.

53

There is reason to believe that its progress in a particular region will be maintained.

54

Measures taken in the running of a certain type of countryside have assisted in the growth of its population.

55

Even though its population has fallen, it can frequently be seen in various particular locations.

56

Winged winners and losers

Birds in Britain come under scrutiny in a massive new study, *Birds Britannica*. A record of the avian community in the 21st century, it reveals a continually evolving pattern. Mark Cocker, the principal author of the tome, selects some cases.

A Red Kite

The red kite's recent rise from a mere handful to several thousands is among the great stories of modern conservation. Testimony to its flagship status is a recent Royal Society for the Protection of Birds poll which ranked it with the golden eagle and song thrush in the nation's list of favourite birds.

The dramatic spread has hinged on a reintroduction scheme at six sites in England and Scotland using kites originally taken from Spain and Sweden. The English releases began in the Chilterns in 1989 and when these had achieved a healthy population, subsequent introductions were made in Northamptonshire and Yorkshire using mainly English birds. The Scottish releases in the 1980s and 1990s have resulted in populations totalling more than 50 pairs. Altogether there are now about 3,000 kites in Britain.

B Dartford Warbler

This highly attractive bird is confined to just five Western European countries as well as the north African littoral, and has the smallest world range of any of our breeding birds. It is also a highly sedentary bird and a major cause of decline is its great susceptibility to the cold. The worst case occurred in the two successive hard winters of 1961 and 1962 when the numbers fell from 450 pairs to just 10.

Memories of this calamitous decrease, coupled with the bird's own tiny size and seeming delicacy, have cemented our sense of an overarching vulnerability. It is one of the best British examples where a species' local rarity has been assumed to equal almost constitutional weakness.

All the caution is perfectly understandable as an expression of our protective instincts towards a much-loved bird. Yet it sits oddly with the warbler's continuing rise and expansion to a population of 1,925 pairs by the year 2000. It has undoubtedly been helped by mild winters as well as the intensive management and protection of England's lowland heath. Yet the Dartford Warbler's recent history illustrates how easy it is to underestimate the resilience of a small rare bird.

C White-tailed Eagle

It is difficult to judge which is the more exciting conservation achievement – the reintroduction of this magnificent bird or of red kites. By wingspan and weight, this is the largest eagle in Europe and one of the biggest of all birds in Britain. However, if the species itself is on a grand scale, the size of the reintroduced population is tiny and the pace of increase agonizingly slow.

The project involved a remarkable team effort by various UK environmental groups, as well as the Norwegian conservationists who organized the capture of the donated birds. Between 1975 and 1985, they released 82 eagles (39 males and 43 females) from a special holding area on the Inner Hebridean island of Rhum. Eight were later recovered dead, but in 1983 came the first breeding attempt.

Two years later, a pair of white-tailed eagles produced the first British-born chick in 69 years and every subsequent breeding season has seen a small incremental improvement. There is now an established breeding nucleus spread between the islands of Skye and Mull as well as the adjacent mainland, and their recent history suggests that the white-tailed eagle's increase will continue throughout north-west Scotland.

D Spotted Flycatcher

Even the greatest fans of this lovely bird, with its mouse-grey upper parts and whitish breast and belly, would have to admit that it is rather drab. They have no more than a thin, squeaky, small song. However, spotted flys compensate with enormous character.

They are adept at catching large species such as day-flying moths, butterflies, bees and wasps, whose stings they remove by thrashing the victim against the perch. Their specialized diet means that they are among the latest spring migrants to return and are now in serious decline because of half a century of pesticide use. In the past 25 years, their numbers have declined by almost 80 per cent, but they are still sufficiently numerous (155,000 pairs) to be familiar and are often birds of large gardens, churchyards or around farm buildings.

Writing (1 hour 30 minutes)

PART 1

You **must** *answer this question. Write your answer in* **220–260** *words in an appropriate style.*

1   You have watched a documentary about what causes young people to start committing crimes. You have made the notes below.

> Reasons why young people commit crimes
> - lack of control by parents
> - absence of opportunities in life
> - influence of friends

> Some opinions expressed in the documentary:
>
> 'Without firm discipline from parents, some children are likely to get into trouble.'
>
> 'It's not surprising that young people who feel they have no chance of a good life turn to crime.'
>
> 'The bad influence of people they mix with can cause some young people to take up crime.'

Write an essay for your tutor discussing two of the reasons in your notes. You should explain which cause you think is the most important for young people committing crimes and provide reasons to support your opinion.

You may, if you wish, make use of the opinions expressed in the documentary, but you should use your own words as far as possible.

Write an answer to **one** *of the questions* **2–4** *in this part. Write your answer in* **220–260** *words in an appropriate style.*

2   You recently spent a week at an adventure sports centre. A friend is thinking of going to the same place and has sent you an email asking about your experiences there. Reply to your friend, giving information and advice. In your email, you should

■   explain what you did at the place
■   describe your feelings during your stay
■   advise your friend about going there.

Write your **email**.

3   You see the following announcement in an international magazine.

LIVE PERFORMANCE REVIEWS WANTED

Have you seen someone perform live who you had previously only heard on recordings or seen on TV or in films? We'd like you to send us reviews of concerts by bands you'd never seen live before or actors you'd never seen on stage. Describe the performance in detail. What did you think and what did the rest of the audience think? Compare the live performance with how the same person / people perform in recordings or on TV or in films. Were they not so good live, or did you prefer them live? Did your opinion of them change? Send your reviews to the address below.

Write your **review**.

4   As part of an exchange programme, you recently spent a week staying in another country with someone who had previously stayed with you as part of the same exchange programme. You have been asked to write a report on your experience. Your report should include where you went and who you stayed with, and what you did during your visit. It should also include a comparison between your visit and the person's previous stay with you, as well as any points you wish to make about the exchange programme in general.

Write your **report**.

Listening (40 minutes)

PART 1

You will hear three different extracts. For questions 1–6, choose the answer (A, B or C) which fits best according to what you hear. There are two questions for each extract.

Extract One
You hear part of a radio programme about a famous London hotel.

1   The presenter's aim in her introduction is to
   A   correct misunderstandings about the Grand.
   B   provide factual information about the Grand.
   C   encourage listeners to go to the Grand.

   [ ] 1

2   What is the manager's attitude towards the customers?
   A   He wishes that more of them were not rich people.
   B   He treats them all in the same way, regardless of who they are.
   C   He always knows instantly what category they belong to.

   [ ] 2

Extract Two
You hear two presenters talking on a science programme.

3   The male presenter says that the research produced data on
   A   the period of time that some teaspoons were missing.
   B   how quickly a certain number of teaspoons disappeared.
   C   where disappearing teaspoons had gone.

   [ ] 3

4   The female presenter says that disappearing teaspoons is a topic which
   A   has produced some interesting theories.
   B   concerns a growing phenomenon.
   C   has no great significance.

   [ ] 4

Extract Three
You hear two people talking about popular music.

5   The woman's main point is that
   A   it is no longer possible to create genuinely original popular music.
   B   all modern popular music is a poor imitation of older music.
   C   popular music has always been an overrated form of music.

   [ ] 5

6   What does the woman say about modern performers?
   A   They are not interested in the views of older people.
   B   They are taking advantage of their audience.
   C   They are influenced without realizing it.

   [ ] 6

PART 2

You will hear part of a talk about best-selling books. For questions 7–14, complete the sentences.

FEATURES OF BEST-SELLING BOOKS

The most popular celebrity autobiographies all focus on the [7] of the celebrity.

Some popular celebrity autobiographies have no [8] in them.

The top-selling cookery books create a sense of [9] that appeals to people.

People who buy the most popular cookery books are most likely to use a recipe from them for [10].

People buy the best-selling sports books because of the [11] in them.

A common feature of popular history books is that they contain [12], which make them interesting to ordinary readers.

Best-selling self-help books now tend to focus on giving advice on how people can make progress with their [13].

In crime fiction, the [14] connected with solving crimes have become a main feature of best-sellers.

You will hear a radio discussion about writing a novel. For questions 15–20, choose the answer (A, B, C or D) which fits best according to what you hear.

15 What does Louise say about Ernest Hemingway's advice to writers?

    A It is useful to a certain extent.
    B It applies only to inexperienced novelists.
    C It wasn't intended to be taken seriously.
    D It might confuse some inexperienced novelists.

    15

16 Louise says that you need to get feedback when you

    A have not been able to write anything for some time.
    B are having difficulty organizing your ideas.
    C are having contrasting feelings about what you have written.
    D have finished the book but not shown it to anyone.

    16

17 Louise says that you should get feedback from another writer because

    A it is easy to ignore criticism from people who are not writers.
    B another writer may be kinder to you than friends and relatives.
    C it is hard to find other people who will make an effort to help you.
    D another writer will understand what your intentions are.

    17

18 What does Louise regard as useful feedback?

    A a combination of general observations and detailed comments
    B both identification of problems and suggested solutions
    C comments focusing more on style than on content
    D as many points about strengths as weaknesses

    18

19 What does Louise say about the people she gets feedback from?

    A Some of them are more successful than her.
    B She doesn't only discuss writing with them.
    C She also gives them feedback on their work.
    D It isn't always easy for her to get together with them.

    19

20 One reaction to feedback that Louise mentions is that

    A it is justified but would require too much effort to act on.
    B it focuses on unimportant details rather than key issues.
    C it has been influenced by reading other people's novels.
    D it is not suggesting that major changes to the novel are required.

    20

TEST 2

PART 4

You will hear five short extracts in which people are talking about events they attended.

Task one

For questions 21–25, choose from the list A–H the event each speaker is talking about.

While you listen you must complete both tasks.

A a concert

B a meeting

C a birthday party

D a school reunion

E a funeral

F a leaving party

G a wedding

H a demonstration

Speaker 1 ___ **21**

Speaker 2 ___ **22**

Speaker 3 ___ **23**

Speaker 4 ___ **24**

Speaker 5 ___ **25**

Task two

For questions 26–30, choose from the list A–H what happened according to each speaker.

A It wasn't well-attended.

B I hardly knew anyone.

C It ended early.

D I was treated badly.

E There was an argument.

F I left before the end.

G Everyone enjoyed themselves.

H I couldn't focus on the event.

Speaker 1 ___ **26**

Speaker 2 ___ **27**

Speaker 3 ___ **28**

Speaker 4 ___ **29**

Speaker 5 ___ **30**

TEST 2

Speaking (15 minutes)

PART 1 (2 minutes)

- Where do you live?

- Who do you live with?

- Why is learning English useful or important to you?

- What reasons do other people have for learning English?

- What kind of technology devices do you own and use regularly?

- What kind of things do you do with your friends?

- How big a part does watching TV play in your life?

- Do you keep a diary? If so, what do you write in it? If not, why not?

- What meals do you have each day, and when?

- How much travelling, within your own country and abroad, have you done?

- What do you like doing the most during your free time? (Why?)

- What household chores do you yourself do at home?

PART 2 (4 minutes)

1 **Glamorous lives**
2 **Learning a skill**

Candidate A	Look at the three pairs of photographs 1A, 1B and 1C on page 47. They show **people with careers that are considered glamorous.**
	Compare two of the pairs of photographs and say **what you think each person's life and personality might be like.**
	Candidate A talks on his / her own for 1 minute.
Candidate B	**Which of the people would you most or least like to be, and why?**
	Candidate B talks on his / her own for about 30 seconds.
Candidate B	Look at the three photographs 2A, 2B and 2C on page 47. They show **people taking classes in order to learn a skill.**
	Compare two of the photographs and say **why the people might be taking the classes, and what might be involved in learning each skill.**
	Candidate B talks on his / her own for 1 minute.
Candidate A	**Which of the skills have you learnt, or would you most like to have, and why?**
	Candidate A talks on his / her own for about 30 seconds.

TEST 2

PART 2

- What do you think the people's lives are like?
- What do you think the people's personalities are like?

1A

1B

1C

- Why might the people be taking the classes?
- What might be involved in learning each skill?

2A

2C

2B

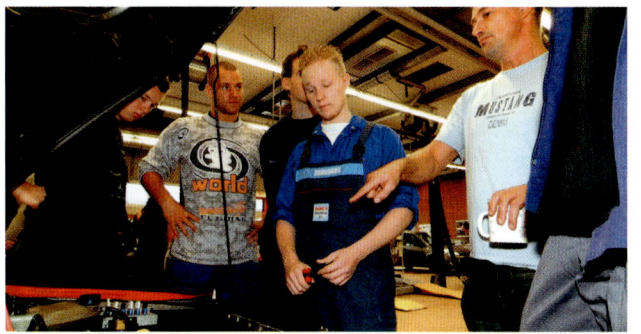

PART 3 (4 minutes) and **PART 4** (5 minutes)

Young people

PART 3

Look at page 49, where there are some issues that young people might care about.

First, talk to each other about **how much young people care about these issues.**

Candidates A and B discuss this together for about 2 minutes.

Now decide **which issue young people in general care about the most.**

Candidates A and B discuss this together for about 1 minute.

PART 4

- Some people say that life is easier today for young people than it used to be. Do you agree? ..... (Why? / Why not?)
- What things do you think that all young people should be able to have and to do?
- What kind of things are expected of young people today, and why? Are these expectations fair? ..... (Why? / Why not?)
- What kind of things can young people learn about life from talking to older people?
- How much influence do you think young people's families have on them? Do you think that their friends have more influence on them? ..... (Why? / Why not?)
- What kind of problems do young people typically have today? What causes these problems?

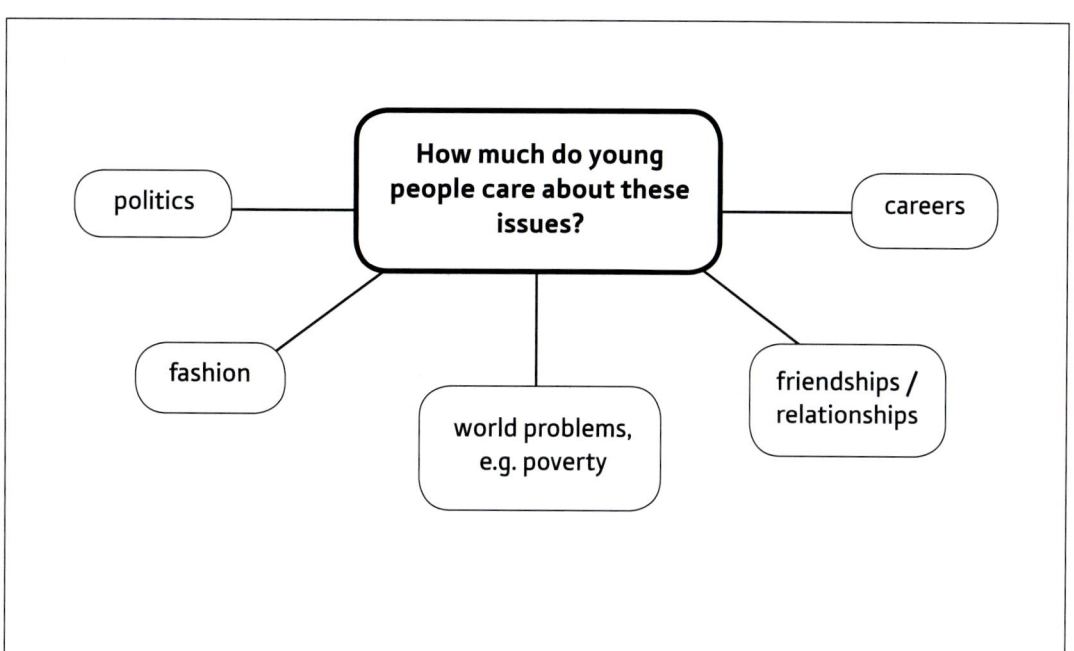

Reading and Use of English (1 hour 30 minutes)

PART 1

For questions 1–8, read the text below and decide which answer (A, B, C or D) best fits each gap. There is an example at the beginning (0).

Mark your answers on the separate answer sheet.

Example:

0   **A** regarded   **B** said   **C** presented   **D** proposed

0	A	B	C	D

Thomas Cook

Thomas Cook could be **0**_____ to have invented the global tourist industry. He was born in England in 1808 and became a cabinet-maker. Then he **1**_____ on the idea of using the newly-invented railways for pleasure trips and by the summer of 1845, he was organizing commercial trips. The first was to Liverpool and featured a 60-page handbook for the journey, the **2**_____ of the modern holiday brochure.

The Paris Exhibition of 1855 **3**_____ him to create his first great tour, taking in France, Belgium and Germany. This also included a remarkable **4**_____ – Cook's first cruise, an extraordinary journey along the Rhine. The expertise he had gained from this **5**_____ him in good stead when it came to organizing a fantastic journey along the Nile in 1869. Few civilians had so much as set foot in Egypt, let **6**_____ travelled along this waterway through history and the remains of a vanished civilization **7**_____ back thousands of years. Then, in 1872, Cook organized the first conducted world tour and the **8**_____ of travel has not been the same since.

1	**A** dawned	**B** struck	**C** hit	**D** crossed
2	**A** pioneer	**B** forerunner	**C** prior	**D** foretaste
3	**A** livened	**B** initiated	**C** launched	**D** inspired
4	**A** breakthrough	**B** leap	**C** step	**D** headway
5	**A** kept	**B** took	**C** stood	**D** made
6	**A** apart	**B** aside	**C** alone	**D** away
7	**A** flowing	**B** going	**C** running	**D** passing
8	**A** scene	**B** area	**C** land	**D** world

For questions **9–16**, read the text below and think of the word which best fits each gap. Use only **one** word in each gap. There is an example at the beginning (**0**).

Write your answers **IN CAPITAL LETTERS** *on the separate answer sheet*.

Example:

0	W	O	U	L	D								

Bits of history (of bits) on the auction block

In the spring of 1946, J. Presper Eckert and John Maunchly sent out a business plan for a company that **0**_____ sell 'electronic computers'. In their eight-page proposal for **9**_____ financing of this enterprise, sent to a small group of prospective backers, the two engineers predicted that the market for **10**_____ a machine might consist **11**_____ scientific laboratories, universities and government agencies. Such **12**_____ the beginnings of the Electronic Control Company of Philadelphia, which produced the Univac, the first computer **13**_____ be commercially sold in the United States.

At an auction around 60 years later, the original typescript of the Eckert-Maunchly proposal was sold as part of a collection called 'The Origins of Cyberspace', which contained about 1,000 books, papers, brochures and **14**_____ artefacts from the history of computing. Two items **15**_____ particular generated interest among prospective bidders. **16**_____ were the Eckert-Maunchly business plan and a technical journal containing the idea for TCP / IP, the standard system for the transmission of information over the Internet.

PART 3

For questions **17–24**, *read the text below. Use the word given in capitals at the end of some of the lines to form a word that fits in the gap* **in the same line**. *There is an example at the beginning* (**0**).

Write your answers **IN CAPITAL LETTERS** *on the separate answer sheet.*

Example:

| 0 | S | T | A | R | D | O | M | | | | | |

ALICIA RHETT – THE STAR WHO ONLY APPEARED IN ONE FILM

Alicia Rhett was an actress who rose to international **0**_____ in the   STAR

1939 film *Gone With the Wind*. In the film, which enjoyed **17**_____   PHENOMENON

success and is among the most popular ever made, she played the

part of India Wilkes, the serious young woman whose love for the

dull and timid **18**_____ character, Charles Hamilton,   CENTRE

is spurned in favour of Scarlett O'Hara. Despite the film's **19**_____   LAST

acclaim, however, it was to be her only screen role.

While Alicia later insisted that she 'enjoyed the experience immensely',

she was **20**_____ to the life of a Hollywood star. An intensely   SUIT

private individual, she lacked the drive and ambition of **21**_____ like   CONTEMPORARY

Joan Crawford or Bette Davis, and went on to reject all subsequent

roles from agents and **22**_____ . Though fans continued to hound   PRODUCE

her with requests for **23**_____ photographs seven decades later,   SIGN

letters went **24**_____ and requests for interviews were seldom   ANSWER

granted.

TEST 3

For questions **25–30**, complete the second sentence so that it has a similar meaning to the first sentence, using the word given. **Do not change the word given.** You must use between **three** and **six** words, including the word given. Here is an example (**0**).

Example:

0 I didn't know the way there, so I got lost.

GET

Not _____ there, I got lost.

0	K N O W I N G H O W T O G E T

*Write **only** the missing words **IN CAPITAL LETTERS** on the separate answer sheet.*

---

25 I've been too busy to answer my emails, but I'll do it soon.

ROUND

I _____ my emails yet, but I'll do it soon.

26 The ambulance came within minutes.

MATTER

It _____ before the ambulance came.

27 Experts say that things are bound to improve.

DOUBT

Experts say that there is _____ better.

28 Jake was the person who started my interest in collecting pottery.

GOT

It _____ in collecting pottery.

29 He really wanted to impress the interviewers.

DESPERATE

He _____ the interviewers a good impression.

30 Because he was injured he couldn't play in the next game.

PREVENTED

His _____ in the next game.

You are going to read an extract from a novel. For questions 31–36, choose the answer (A, B, C or D) which you think fits best according to the text.

Mark your answers on the separate answer sheet.

Thirty or so years after he arrived in London, Chanu decided that it was time to see the sights. 'All I saw was the Houses of Parliament. And that was in 1979.' It was a project. Much equipment was needed. Preparations were made. Chanu bought a pair of shorts which hung just below his knees. He tried them on and filled the numerous pockets with a compass, guidebook, binoculars, bottled water, maps and two types of disposable camera. Thus loaded, the shorts hung at mid-calf. He bought a baseball cap and wore it around the flat with the visor variously angled up and down and turned around to the back of his head. A money belt secured the shorts around his waist and prevented them from reaching his ankles. He made a list of tourist attractions and devised a star rating system that encompassed historical significance, something he termed 'entertainment factor' and value for money. The girls would enjoy themselves. They were forewarned of this requirement.

On a hot Saturday morning towards the end of July the planning came to fruition. 'I've spent more than half my life here,' said Chanu, 'but I've hardly left these few streets.' He stared out of the bus windows at the grimy colours of Bethnal Green Road. 'All this time I have been struggling and struggling, and I've barely had time to lift my head and look around.'

They sat at the front of the bus, on the top deck. Chanu shared a seat with Nazneen, and Shahana and Bibi sat across the aisle. Nazneen crossed her ankles and tucked her feet beneath the seat to make way for the two plastic carrier bags that contained their picnic. 'You'll stink the bus out,' Shahana had said. 'I'm not sitting with you.' But she had not moved away.

'It's like this,' said Chanu, 'when you have all the time in the world to see something, you don't bother to see it. Now that we are going home, I have become a tourist.' He pulled his sunglasses from his forehead onto his nose. They were part of the new equipment.

He turned to the girls. 'How do you like your holiday so far?' Bibi said that she liked it very well, and Shahana squinted and shuffled and leaned her head against the side window.

Chanu began to hum. He danced with his head, which wobbled from side to side, and drummed out a rhythm on his thigh. The humming appeared to come from low down in his chest and melded with the general tune of the bus, vibrating on the bass notes.

Nazneen decided that she would make this day unlike any other. She would not allow this day to disappoint him.

The conductor came to collect fares. He had a slack-jawed expression: nothing could interest him. 'Two at one pound, and two children, please,' said Chanu. He received his tickets. 'Sightseeing,' he announced, and flourished his guidebook. 'Family holiday.'

'Right,' said the conductor. He jingled his bag, looking for change. He was squashed by his job. The ceiling forced him to stoop.

'Can you tell me something? To your mind, does the British Museum rate more highly than the National Gallery? Or would you recommend the gallery over the museum?'

The conductor pushed his lower lip out with his tongue. He stared hard at Chanu, as if considering whether to eject him from the bus.

'In my rating system,' explained Chanu, 'they are neck and neck. It would be good to take an opinion from a local.'

'Where've you come from, mate?'

'Oh, just two blocks behind,' said Chanu. 'But this is the first holiday for twenty or thirty years.'

The conductor swayed. It was still early but the bus was hot and Nazneen could smell his sweat. He looked at Chanu's guidebook. He twisted round and looked at the girls. At a half-glance he knew everything about Nazneen, and then he shook his head and walked away.

31 In what sense was the sightseeing trip a 'project' (line 4)?

   A Chanu felt a duty to do it.
   B It was something that Chanu had wanted to do for a long time.
   C Chanu took it very seriously.
   D It was something that required a good deal of organization.

31

32 The descriptions of Chanu's clothing are intended to

   A show how little he cared about his appearance.
   B create an impression of his sense of humour.
   C create amusing visual images of him.
   D show how bad his choice of clothes always was.

32

33 Chanu had decided to go on a sightseeing trip that day because

   A he regretted the lack of opportunity to do so before.
   B he felt that it was something the girls ought to do.
   C he had just developed an interest in seeing the sights.
   D he had grown bored with the area that he lived in.

33

34 As they sat on top of the bus,

   A Nazneen began to regret bringing so much food with them.
   B the girls felt obliged to pretend that they were enjoying themselves.
   C Chanu explained why he had brought the whole family on the trip.
   D the family members showed different amounts of enthusiasm for the trip.

34

35 When Chanu showed him the guidebook, the conductor

   A made it clear that he wanted to keep moving through the bus.
   B appeared to think that Chanu might cause a problem.
   C initially pretended not to have heard what Chanu said.
   D felt that he must have misunderstood what Chanu said.

35

36 What was strange about Chanu's use of the word 'local'?

   A It was not relevant to the places he was asking about.
   B It could equally have been applied to him.
   C He was not using it with its normal meaning.
   D He had no reason to believe it applied to the conductor.

36

You are going to read four extracts from biographies of a former political leader. For questions 37–40, choose from the biographies A–D. The biographies may be chosen more than once.

Mark your answers on the separate answer sheet.

A career at the very top of the political ladder
Four biographers assess one national leader's political career

A

The overall impression one gets of him is of someone whose true ambitions lay outside politics, and for whom political leadership was more of a CV item than a duty born of a desire to serve his country. A shrewd and manipulative operator, he knew how to make the right alliances to get himself into the positions he wanted, and once his term of office was over he continued in that vein outside politics. The legacy of his time in office is a contrasting one. Top of the list in the plus column is the tremendous progress he made in narrowing the gap between rich and poor as a result of policies he personally championed against considerable opposition. Less creditable is the fact that many of the problems that resulted from his time in office can be laid at his door too and there were repercussions he should have foreseen.

B

Seldom can a political leader be said to have been such a victim of bad timing. Many of his policies made complete sense in themselves and at almost any other time would have had a positive impact, but circumstances beyond his control conspired to turn them into disasters for the country. It could perhaps be said that this was made worse by the fact that he was somewhat gullible, setting far too much store by the questionable advice of key figures around him. He rose to power with a sincere belief that he could improve the lives of people at every level of society, although it could be said that self-interest later guided him more than this initial desire. Probably the most positive thing that can be said about his term of office is that he minimized the impact of some tough economic times, steering the country through them with reasonable success, which was no mean feat.

C

Views differ widely on what sort of man he was as a leader, with conflicting testimony from those on the inside. What emerges is someone who appeared decisive but who in reality tended to believe what he was told by trusted advisers and experts, and was too easily swayed by them. His unquestioning faith in such people led him to try to implement changes that were far too radical for the time and it is fair to say that he was at fault for going along with this approach that was advocated by others. On the positive side, his main achievement was to make the country more competitive economically by means of some well-considered initiatives, though these later turned out to have only short-term impact. This reflected the commitment to modernize the country that had been at the centre of his campaign and the reason why he had aspired to the leadership in the first place.

D

He was driven to the top by a genuine belief that he knew best and that his critics were incapable of seeing that his policies would indeed produce very real improvements across the board. Though he made a show of listening to advice from others, he was in reality inflexible. This led him to continue to pursue policies that were manifestly not working and he should have accepted that a change of direction was required. He had one of the sharpest minds of any leader in recent history, and an ability to analyse situations forensically, but at key times he failed to apply these qualities and carried on regardless of the inadvisability of doing so. Nevertheless, he succeeded in one major way: he made society more equal and in so doing improved the lot of many of the less well-off members of it.

Which biographer

has a different opinion from the others on the extent to which the subject was personally responsible for problems caused by his policies?

[ ] **37**

shares biographer D's view on the subject's personal characteristics as a leader?

[ ] **38**

differs from the others on the subject's motivation for becoming a political leader?

[ ] **39**

expresses a similar view to biographer A on what the subject's greatest achievement was?

[ ] **40**

PART 7

You are going to read a newspaper article about singing in choirs. Six paragraphs have been removed from the article. Choose from the paragraphs A–G the one which fits each gap (41–46). There is one extra paragraph which you do not need to use.

Mark your answers on the separate answer sheet.

Introducing choral music to children is like opening a door to a magical world

Here's an important question. What's calming, therapeutic, healthier than drugs, and could well prolong your life? Answer: singing in a choir.

41

In fairness, there was a specific angle to this study, which compared the collective experience of choral singing to that of taking part in team sports. Choirs apparently win hands down, because there's 'a stronger sense of being part of a meaningful group', related to 'the synchronicity of moving and breathing with other people'. And as someone who since childhood has used singing as a refuge from the sports field, I take no issue with that.

42

I know there are occasional initiatives. From time to time I get invited as a music critic to the launch of some scheme or other to encourage more collective singing among school-age children. There are smiles and brave words. Then, six months later, everything goes quiet – until the next launch of the next initiative.

43

I know a woman who's been trying hard to organize a performance of Benjamin Britten's *Noye's Fludde* – perhaps the greatest work ever devised for young children to sing together – as a tribute to the composer's centenary this year. But has she found her local schools responsive? Sadly not: it was all too much trouble.

44

We sang Herbert Howells's *Like as the Hart*. And whatever it did or didn't do for my cardiovascular system, my emotional health, or any of the other things that turn up in research papers, it was the most significant experience of my childhood. It opened a world to which 11-year-olds from unfashionable parts of east London don't generally get access. It was magical, transcendent. It spoke possibilities.

45

The other weekend I was in Suffolk, celebrating Britten, where in fact there were a lot of children privileged enough to be pulled into the centenary events. There was a great *Noye's Fludde* in Lowestoft. And on the actual birthday countless hordes of infant voices piled into Snape Maltings to sing Britten's school songs, *Friday Afternoons*, part of a project that involved 100,000 others, internationally, doing likewise.

46

Just think: if we could finally get Britain's children singing, it would filter upwards. And we wouldn't need university researchers. We'd just do it, and be all the better for it.

A It was an extraordinary experience that many of those children will carry with them all their lives, like my experience all those years ago. There's a plan for it to be repeated every year on Britten's birthday. But that will only happen if there are resources and sustained commitment (for a change).

B In fact, I have no argument with any of these piles of research – bring them on, the more the better – because what they have to say is true. The only thing I find annoying is that such an endlessly repeated truth results in relatively little action from the kind of people who could put it to good use.

C One of my enduring life regrets is that I never got the chance to take part in such an event as a child. I guess I went to schools where it was also too much trouble. But I did, just once, aged 11, get the chance to go with a choir and sing at Chelmsford Cathedral.

D But being there was even better. And as I was sitting near the choir – who were magnificent – I saw the faces of the boys and thought how fabulously privileged they were to have this opportunity given to them.

E And that, for me, is what a choir can offer. All the physical and mental pluses are a happy bonus. But the joy and thrill of access to that world of music is what counts.

F It's not a new discovery: there are endless dissertations on the subject, libraries of research, and celebrity endorsements. But people have short memories. So every time another academic paper is published, it gets into the news – which was what happened this week when Oxford Brookes University came up with the latest 'singing is good for you' revelation.

G The hard fact is that most state schools don't bother much with singing, unless someone in the hierarchies of government steps in to make it worth their while. They say they don't have the resources or the time. And even when a worthwhile singing project drops into their lap, they turn it down.

*You are going to read an article about various paintings. For questions **47–56**, choose from the paintings (**A–D**). The paintings may be chosen more than once.*

*Mark your answers **on the separate answer sheet**.*

Of which painting are the following stated?

It is of something that no longer exists.	47
The artist points out that it is based on things actually observed, even though it doesn't depict them accurately.	48
The artist specializes in things that most people regard as ugly.	49
A deduction that could be made about what is happening in it is not what the artist is actually showing.	50
The artist took a risk while creating it.	51
The artist checks that nothing important is missing from preparatory work.	52
It was completely altered in order to produce various connections.	53
Its artist produces paintings in different locations.	54
In one way, it is unlike any other painting the artist has produced.	55
The artist likes to find by chance subjects that have certain characteristics.	56

Watercolour competition

THE WINNERS

First prize

A Carol Robertson *Interrupted Field*

Carol Robertson's Interrupted Field is a worthy winner, a more or less geometric composition that exploits the qualities of evenly-applied washes of colour. The painting is vast – 'the largest I've ever attempted' – so the big, even area of blue in the centre is, apart from anything else, something of a technical achievement.

Robertson is keen to stress that her abstract compositions are firmly rooted in reality. Though she doesn't 'seek to confirm or record the way the world looks', her work is never disconnected from the natural world, so the coloured stripes and bands in this painting have a specific source. Over the past five years, Robertson has been working in Ireland, on the northwest coast of County Mayo. The coloured stripes stimulate 'memories of coastal landscape, brightly painted cottages, harbours and fishing boats, things seen out of the corner of my eye as I explored that coastline by car and on foot. The colour mirrors the fragments of life that caught my eye against a background of sea and sky.'

Runners up

B Geoffrey Wynne *Quayside*

Geoffrey Wynne describes himself as 'an open-air impressionist watercolour painter', though he adds that 'larger works', this prize-winning picture among them, 'are developed in the studio'.

Perhaps the most noteworthy aspect of this painting is the sheer number of people in it. According to the title, they are on a quay somewhere, and the number of suitcases they have with them suggests they have just landed from a boat on the first stage of a holiday. 'Yes, that's almost right,' Wynne told me, 'except that we're on the boat in the early morning, just arrived back from Mallorca, and the people are waiting to get on. This painting took a long time to finish, and many earlier attempts were abandoned. To achieve a unity, I immersed the half-finished painting in the bath, then added the black with a big brush. It's dangerous to do, because you can't really control the effects. Then I reworked everything, establishing links with colour and tone throughout the composition, creating a kind of web or net of similar effects.'

C Arthur Lockwood *Carbonizer Tower*

Arthur Lockwood has a big reputation among watercolour painters and watercolour enthusiasts, chiefly for his accomplished pictures of industrial sites, subjects that are generally thought to be unsightly, but have striking visual qualities all their own. Among them is a kind of romanticism stimulated by indications of

decay and the passing of irrecoverable time. Lockwood's subjects are, after all, ruins, the modern equivalent of Gothic churches overgrown by ivy. He aims not only to reveal those qualities, but to make a visual record of places that are fast being destroyed. This painting, a good example of his work in general, is one of an extensive series on the same subject. What we see is part of a large industrial plant that once made smokeless coal briquettes. It has now been closed and demolished to make way for a business park.

D Michael Smee *Respite at The Royal Oak*

Michael Smee was once a successful stage and television designer. This is worth stressing, because this prize-winning painting makes a strong theatrical impression. Smee agrees, and thinks it has much to do with the carefully judged lighting. 'As a theatre designer, you make the set, which comes to life only when it's lit.'

Smee prefers to happen on pubs and cafés that are intriguing visually and look as though they might be under threat. He has a strong desire to record 'not only the disappearing pub culture peculiar to this country, but also bespoke bar interiors and the individuals therein'. He works his paintings up from informative sketches. 'I get there early, before many people have arrived, sit in the corner and scribble away. Then, once the painting is in progress in the studio, I make a return visit to reassure myself and to note down what I'd previously overlooked.' His main aim isn't topographical accuracy, however; it's to capture the appearance of artificial and natural light together, as well as the reflections they make.

Writing (1 hour 30 minutes)

PART 1

*You **must** answer this question. Write your answer in 220–260 words in an appropriate style.*

1 Your class has attended a panel discussion on what are the greatest advantages of digital and computer technology for people in their everyday lives. You have made the notes below.

> Advantages of digital and computer technology in everyday life
>
> • communication
>
> • access to information
>
> • shopping and services

> Some opinions expressed in the discussion:
>
> 'Being able to contact anyone at any time in any place is obviously the greatest advantage.'
>
> 'The fact that people can instantly look up something and find out about it, or learn something new, is the greatest advantage.'
>
> 'You don't need to go out or spend a long time buying or paying for things and that's the greatest advantage.'

Write an essay for your tutor discussing **two** of the advantages in your notes. You should **explain which advantage you think is the greatest** for people in their everyday lives and **provide reasons** to support your opinion.

You may, if you wish, make use of the opinions expressed in the discussion, but you should use your own words as far as possible.

Write an answer to one of the questions 2–4 in this part. Write your answer in 220–260 words in an appropriate style.

2   You have seen this announcement in an international magazine.

> **The local council has created a new fund to provide financial assistance to people setting up new small businesses.**
>
> Anyone wishing to set up a business but lacking the funds to do so is invited to send a proposal for their business to the relevant department of the council, giving details of what it would involve, how it would be set up and what the funds would be used for.

Write your **proposal**.

3   As a member of the entertainments committee at the place where you work or study, you have been asked to write a report on the events that the committee organized over the past year. In your report, you should describe events that took place and what they involved, say whether they were successful or not, and comment on the organization of them.

Write your **report**.

4   You have just returned from a trip during which you rented an apartment for a week. You were very pleased with the accommodation and you have decided to write a review of it for a travel website. In your review, describe your experience of renting the apartment, say what the apartment was like, and explain why you enjoyed your stay there.

Write your **review**.

Listening (40 minutes)

PART 1

You will hear three different extracts. For questions 1–6, choose the answer (A, B or C) which fits best according to what you hear. There are two questions for each extract.

Extract One
You hear two people talking about reading books aloud for children.

1 The second speaker says that she believes that

   A her children enjoy listening to her read aloud.
   B she shares a reading habit with other parents.
   C parents should read aloud to children.

   `1`

2 What do both speakers talk about?

   A their children's reactions when they read aloud to them
   B their selfish motives for reading aloud to their children
   C their dramatic approach to reading aloud to their children

   `2`

Extract Two
You hear a part of a radio programme.

3 The presenter says that some people start a business with a friend because

   A they have worked well together in the past.
   B their friend persuades them to do it.
   C they lack the courage to do it alone.

   `3`

4 What was Dean's problem with his partner?

   A He refused to take part in an important aspect of the business.
   B His personality changed after they started the business.
   C He often criticized the business decisions Dean made.

   `4`

Extract Three
You hear two people on a radio programme talking about running.

5 Who are the two speakers?

   A successful athletes
   B fitness experts
   C sports journalists

   `5`

6 Both speakers agree that, to improve as a runner, runners should

   A limit the amount of training they do.
   B develop their own personal training methods.
   C vary the focus of their training.

   `6`

You will hear someone who works as a life coach talking about her work.
For questions 7–14, complete the sentences with a word or short phrase.

BEING A LIFE COACH

The speaker tells people who ask her that her work is connected with the
[7   ] .

The speaker says that most people concentrate too much on what she calls their
'[8   ] '.

The speaker calls the plan to achieve a specific goal a '[9   ] '.

The speaker gives as an example of a personal goal increasing your ability at
[10   ] .

The speaker gives as an example of a business goal thinking of new
[11   ] .

The speaker says that sessions are conducted in a way that prevents any
[12   ] .

The speaker says that sessions do not involve dealing with a person's
[13   ] .

The speaker says that life coaches enable people to become [14   ]
themselves.

You will hear a radio discussion about children who invent imaginary friends. For questions 15–20, choose the answer (A, B, C or D) which fits best according to what you hear.

15 In the incident that Liz describes,
   A her daughter asked her to stop the car.
   B she had to interrupt the journey twice.
   C she got angry with her daughter.
   D her daughter wanted to get out of the car.

   15

16 What does the presenter say about the latest research into imaginary friends?
   A It contradicts other research on the subject.
   B It shows that the number of children who have them is increasing.
   C It indicates that negative attitudes towards them are wrong.
   D It focuses on the effect they have on parents.

   16

17 How did Liz feel when her daughter had an imaginary friend?
   A always confident that it was only a temporary situation
   B occasionally worried about the friend's importance to her daughter
   C slightly confused as to how she should respond sometimes
   D highly impressed by her daughter's inventiveness

   17

18 Karen says that one reason why children have imaginary friends is that
   A they are having serious problems with their real friends.
   B they can tell imaginary friends what to do.
   C they want something that they cannot be given.
   D they want something that other children haven't got.

   18

19 Karen says that the teenager who had invented a superhero is an example of
   A a very untypical teenager.
   B a problem that imaginary friends can cause.
   C something she had not expected to discover.
   D how children change as they get older.

   19

20 According to Karen, how should parents react to imaginary friends?
   A They should pretend that they like the imaginary friend.
   B They shouldn't get involved in the child's relationship with the friend.
   C They should take action if the situation becomes annoying.
   D They shouldn't discuss the imaginary friend with their child.

   20

PART 4

You will hear five short extracts in which people are talking about the music industry.

Task one

For questions 21–25, choose from the list A–H who is speaking.

Task two

For questions 26–30, choose from the list A–H the opinion each speaker expresses.

While you listen you must complete both tasks.

A	a recording studio engineer	
B	a musician	
C	a reviewer	Speaker 1 [ ] **21**
D	a club owner	Speaker 2 [ ] **22**
E	a fan	Speaker 3 [ ] **23**
F	a website operator	Speaker 4 [ ] **24**
G	a manager of performers	Speaker 5 [ ] **25**
H	a radio presenter	

A	Tastes in music change very quickly.	
B	Music is an important part of culture.	
C	Some people who become well-known don't deserve their success.	Speaker 1 [ ] **26**
D	There are lots of dishonest people in the music business.	Speaker 2 [ ] **27**
E	Artists need to have a realistic view of the music business.	Speaker 3 [ ] **28**
F	People with real talent will always succeed.	Speaker 4 [ ] **29**
G	Some artists will always be popular.	Speaker 5 [ ] **30**
H	People should only get involved in music because they love it.	

TEST 3

Speaking (15 minutes)

PART 1 (2 minutes)

- How did you get here today?
- How do you normally travel to the place where you work or study?
- How have you been learning English?
- What aspects of learning English have you found most and least enjoyable? ..... (Why?)

- What are your main sources of entertainment?
- What kind of films do you enjoy? ..... (Why?)
- How do you normally communicate with friends and family?
- Would you say that you have a healthy lifestyle? ..... (Why? / Why not?)
- What kind of news do you keep up to date with?
- Do you like parties? If so, what kind of parties do you like most? If not, why not?
- Which person / people do you usually see every day?
- Do you have a lot of free time? (Why / Why not?)

PART 2 (4 minutes)

1 Running
2 Speaking in public

Candidate A	Look at the three photographs 1A, 1B and 1C on page 69. They show people running.
	Compare two of the photographs and say why the people might be running, and what kind of lives they may have.
	Candidate A talks on his / her own for 1 minute.
Candidate B	Which of the pictures is closest to something you have done or experienced, and why?
	Candidate B talks on his / her own for about 30 seconds.
Candidate B	Look at the three photographs 2A, 2B and 2C on page 69. They show people speaking in public.
	Compare two of the photographs and say **what the people might be talking about, and what the situation might be.**
	Candidate B talks on his / her own for 1 minute.
Candidate A	Which of the speakers would you prefer to listen to, and why?
	Candidate A talks on his / her own for about 30 seconds.

TEST 3

PART 2

- Why do you think the people are running?
- What do you think the people's lives are like?

1A

1B

1C

- What do you think the speakers are talking about?
- What do you think the situation is?

2A

2B

2C

PART 3 (4 minutes) and PART 4 (5 minutes)

Environmental issues

PART 3

Look at page 71, where there are some **environmental** problems.

First, talk to each other about **how easy or difficult it is to find solutions to these environmental problems.**

Candidates A and B discuss this together for about 2 minutes.

Now decide **which issue is the easiest one to solve.**

Candidates A and B discuss this together for about 1 minute.

PART 4

- Some people say that the environment is the biggest issue in the modern world. Do you agree? Do you think there are more important issues?
- What impact can individuals have concerning environmental issues? What do you do personally that is connected with environmental issues?
- Do you think that people in general are concerned about the environment? If so, what concerns them most? If not, why not?
- Are people given enough information about environmental problems? Where do they get their information from?
- Many companies today advertise the ways in which they are environmentally friendly. Is this a positive development or does it have little effect?
- What should governments be doing about environmental problems?

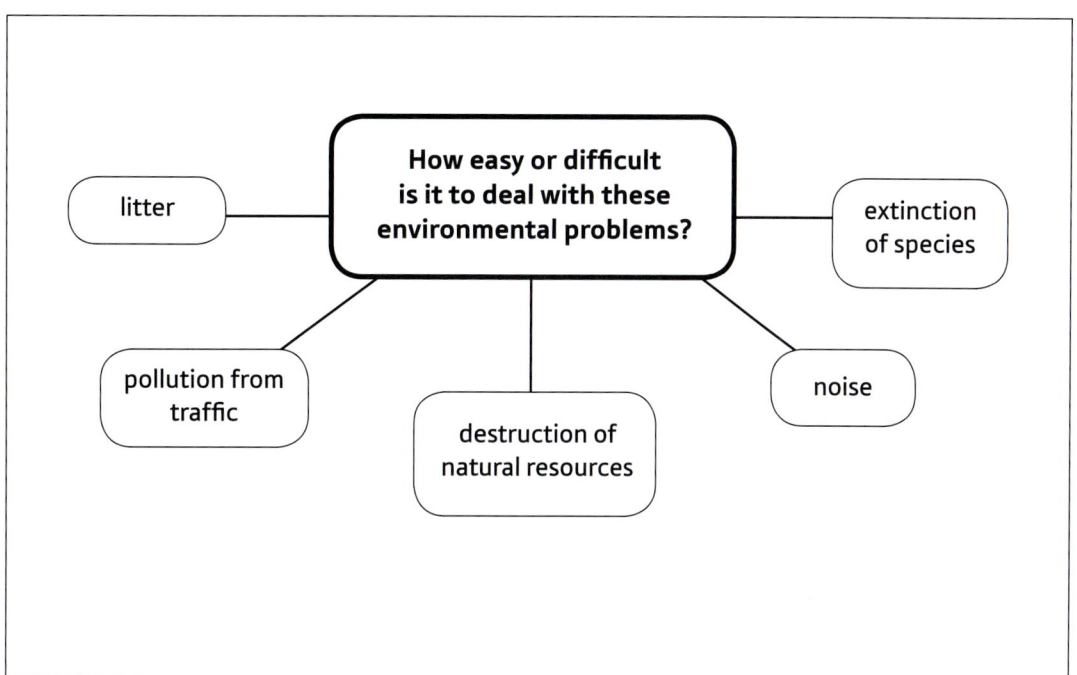

TEST 3

Reading and Use of English (1 hour 30 minutes)

PART 1

For questions 1–8, read the text below and decide which answer (A, B, C or D) best fits each gap. There is an example at the beginning (0).

Mark your answers on the separate answer sheet.

Example:

0 **A** characterized   **B** indicated   **C** detailed   **D** accounted

0	A	B	C	D

High notes of the singing Neanderthals

Neanderthals have been misunderstood. The early humanoids traditionally **0**_____ as ape-like brutes were deeply emotional beings with high-pitched voices. They may **1**_____ have sung to each other. This new image has **2**_____ from two studies of the vocal apparatus and anatomy of the creatures that **3**_____ Europe between 200,000 and 35,000 years ago.

The research shows that Neanderthal voices might well have produced loud, womanly and highly melodic sounds – not the roars and grunts previously **4**_____ by most researchers. Stephen Mithen, Professor of Archaeology

and author of one of the studies, said: 'What is emerging is a picture of an intelligent and emotionally complex creature whose most likely **5**_____ of communication would have been part language and part song.'

Mithen's work **6**_____ with the first detailed study of a reconstructed Neanderthal skeleton. Anthropologists brought together bones and casts from several sites to re-create the creature. The creature that emerges would have **7**_____ markedly from humans. Neanderthals seem to have had an extremely powerful **8**_____ and no waist.

1	**A** further	**B** just	**C** even	**D** so
2	**A** revealed	**B** resulted	**C** concluded	**D** happened
3	**A** resided	**B** dwelt	**C** filled	**D** occupied
4	**A** judged	**B** assumed	**C** considered	**D** taken
5	**A** sort	**B** practice	**C** approach	**D** form
6	**A** coincides	**B** occurs	**C** relates	**D** co-operates
7	**A** differed	**B** distinguished	**C** compared	**D** contrasted
8	**A** assembly	**B** formation	**C** build	**D** scheme

For questions **9–16**, read the text below and think of the word which best fits each gap. Use only **one** word in each gap. There is an example at the beginning (**0**).

Write your answers **IN CAPITAL LETTERS** *on the separate answer sheet*.

Example:

0	P	L	A	C	E								

WORLD BOOK DAY

This year's World Book Day (WBD), which is taking **0**_____ on March 2, hopes to encourage everyone, and especially children, to discover the joy of reading.

Schools and libraries are getting involved, with a packed schedule of events designed **9**_____ bring books to life. There will be writers popping **10**_____ schools to read from their books and answer questions, and story-telling events. Children will also be able to take part in readings **11**_____ that they really have a chance to engage with the books.

As **12**_____ as hoping to encourage children to catch the reading bug, WBD also hopes to **13**_____ reluctant adults hooked on books. So, **14**_____ the first time, World Book Day will also have an adult focus, with the launch of Quick Reads, **15**_____ selection of short, fast-paced stories by well-known authors. The first set of Quick Reads will be published on World Book Day, **16**_____ a further collection of books being released later in the summer.

PART 3

For questions **17–24**, *read the text below. Use the word given in capitals at the end of some of the lines to form a word that fits in the gap* **in the same line**. *There is an example at the beginning* (**0**).

Write your answers **IN CAPITAL LETTERS** *on the separate answer sheet.*

Example:

| 0 | E | F | F | E | C | T | I | V | E | | | | |

NORDIC WALKING

Nordic walking is an **0**_____ technique that uses poles to bring   EFFECT

the upper body into more use and boost the calorie-burning effects of

walking. It was **17**_____ devised in Finland by elite cross-country   ORIGIN

skiers as a way to keep their fitness levels up during the summer.

   At first **18**_____ , Nordic walking may look like skiing without the   SEE

skis – or the snow. But although, to the **19**_____ eye, striding around   TRAIN

the local park with a pair of poles may look a bit silly, it actually offers a

serious **20**_____ for people of all ages and abilities. You don't   WORK

21_____ have to go faster to get more out of it – just put in more effort   NECESSARY

with the poles. The poles, which can be made from aluminium or carbon

fibre, are specially designed to **22**_____ the work done by the upper   MAXIMUM

body. And because Nordic walking is also a weight-bearing exercise, it's

great for **23**_____ bones and joints. But the best news is that because   STRONG

the effort is spread across the **24**_____ of the body, Nordic walking can   ENTIRE

actually feel easier and less tiring than normal walking.

PART 4

For questions **25–30**, complete the second sentence so that it has a similar meaning to the first sentence, using the word given. **Do not change the word given.** You must use between **three** and **six** words, including the word given. Here is an example (**0**).

Example:

0 I didn't know the way there, so I got lost.

GET

Not _____ there, I got lost.

0	K N O W I N G H O W T O G E T

Write *only the missing words* **IN CAPITAL LETTERS** *on the separate answer sheet*.

---

25 Can anyone solve this problem?

COME

Can anyone _____ to this problem?

26 I'm sure you're wondering why I haven't contacted you for so long.

HAS

You must _____ so long since I contacted you.

27 Are you saying that I'm lying about what happened?

TRUTH

Are you accusing _____ about what happened?

28 He made a very quick decision and he didn't think about the matter enough.

WITHOUT

He made a very quick decision _____ to the matter.

29 Recently, the number of people who are out of work has gone down.

DECREASE

Recently, _____ the number of people who are out of work.

30 It doesn't matter how badly he behaved, you shouldn't have been so rude to him.

HOWEVER

You shouldn't have been so rude to him, _____ was.

You are going to read a newspaper article about trees and leaves. For questions 31–36, choose the answer (A, B, C or D) which you think fits best according to the text.

Mark your answers *on the separate answer sheet*.

Those brilliant autumn outfits may be saving trees

As trees across the northern areas of the globe turn gold and crimson, scientists are debating exactly what these colours are for. The scientists do agree on one thing: the colours are for something. That represents a major shift in thinking. For decades, textbooks claimed that autumn colours were just a by-product of dying leaves. 'I had always assumed that autumn leaves were waste baskets,' said Dr. David Wilkinson, an evolutionary ecologist at Liverpool John Moores University in England. 'That's what I was told as a student.'

During spring and summer, leaves get their green cast from chlorophyll, the pigment that plays a major role in capturing sunlight. But the leaves also contain other pigments whose colours are masked during the growing season. In autumn, trees break down their chlorophyll and draw some of the components back into their tissues. Conventional wisdom regards autumn colours as the product of the remaining pigments, which are finally unmasked.

Evolutionary biologists and plant physiologists offer two different explanations for why natural selection has made autumn colours so widespread. Dr. William Hamilton, an evolutionary biologist at Oxford University, proposed that bright autumn leaves contain a message: they warn insects to leave them alone. Dr. Hamilton's 'leaf signal' hypothesis grew out of earlier work he had done on the extravagant plumage of birds. He proposed it served as an advertisement from males to females, indicating they had desirable genes. As females evolved

a preference for those displays, males evolved more extravagant feathers as they competed for mates. In the case of trees, Dr. Hamilton proposed that the visual message was sent to insects. In the autumn, aphids and other insects choose trees where they will lay their eggs. When the eggs hatch the next spring, the larvae feed on the tree, often with devastating results. A tree can ward off these pests with poisons. Dr. Hamilton speculated that trees with strong defences might be able to protect themselves even further by letting egg-laying insects know what was in store for their eggs. By producing brilliant autumn colours, the trees advertised their lethality. As insects evolved to avoid the brightest leaves, natural selection favoured trees that could become even brighter.

'It was a beautiful idea,' said Marco Archetti, a former student of Dr. Hamilton who is now at the University of Fribourg in Switzerland. Dr. Hamilton had Mr. Archetti turn the hypothesis into a mathematical model. The model showed that warning signals could indeed drive the evolution of bright leaves – at least in theory. Another student, Sam Brown, tested the leaf-signal hypothesis against real data about trees and insects. 'It was a first stab to see what was out there,' said Dr. Brown, now an evolutionary biologist at the University of Texas.

The leaf-signal hypothesis has also drawn criticism, most recently from Dr. Wilkinson and Dr. H. Martin Schaefer, an evolutionary biologist at the University of Freiburg in Germany. Dr. Wilkinson and other critics point to a number of details

about aphids and trees that do not fit Dr. Hamilton's hypothesis. Dr. William Hoch, a plant physiologist at the University of Wisconsin, argues that bright leaves appear on trees that have no insects to warn off. 'If you are up here in the north of Wisconsin, by the time the leaves change, all the insects that feed on foliage are gone,' Dr. Hoch said. In their article, Dr. Schaefer and Dr. Wilkinson argue that a much more plausible explanation for autumn colours can be found in the research of Dr. Hoch and other plant physiologists. Their recent work suggests that autumn colours serve mainly as a sunscreen.

Dr. Hamilton's former students argue that the leaf-signal hypothesis is still worth investigating. Dr. Brown believes that leaves might be able to protect themselves both from sunlight and from insects. Dr. Brown and Dr. Archetti also argue that supporters of the sunscreen hypothesis have yet to explain why some trees have bright colours and some do not. 'This is a basic question in evolution that they seem to ignore,' Dr. Archetti said. 'I don't think it's a huge concern,' Dr. Hoch replied. 'There's natural variation for every characteristic.'

Dr. Hamilton's students and their critics agree that the debate has been useful, because it has given them a deeper reverence for this time of year. 'People sometimes say that science makes the world less interesting and awesome by just explaining things away,' Dr. Wilkinson said. 'But with autumn leaves, the more you know about them, the more amazed you are.'

31 What is stated about the colours of autumn leaves in the first two paragraphs?
   A There has previously been no disagreement about what causes them.
   B The process that results in them has never been fully understood.
   C Different colours from those that were previously the norm have started to appear.
   D Debate about the purpose of them has gone on for a long time,

   `31`

32 The writer says that Dr Hamilton's work has focused on
   A the different purposes of different colours.
   B the use of colour for opposite purposes.
   C the possibility that birds and insects have influenced each other's behaviour.
   D the increased survival rates of certain kinds of tree.

   `32`

33 Dr Hamilton has suggested that there is a connection between
   A the colours of autumn leaves and the behaviour of insects.
   B the development of brighter leaves and the reduced numbers of certain
      types of insect.
   C the survival of trees and the proximity of insects to them.
   D the brightness of leaves and the development of other defence mechanisms in trees.

   `33`

34 What is said about the work done by former students of Dr Hamilton?
   A Neither of them was able to achieve what they set out to do.
   B Mr Archetti felt some regret about the outcome of the work he did.
   C Both of them initiated the idea of doing the work.
   D Dr Brown did not expect to draw any firm conclusions from his work.

   `34`

35 Critics of Dr Hamilton's theory have expressed the view that
   A it is impossible to generalize about the purpose of the colours of autumn leaves.
   B his theory is based on a misunderstanding about insect behaviour.
   C the colours of autumn leaves have a different protective function.
   D his theory can only be applied to certain kinds of insect.

   `35`

36 In the debate between the two groups of people investigating the subject, it has been
   suggested that
   A something regarded as a key point by one side is in fact not important.
   B further research will prove that Dr Hamilton's theory is the correct one.
   C both sides may in fact be completely wrong.
   D the two sides should collaborate.

   `36`

TEST 4

You are going to read four extracts from articles on freelance work. For questions 37–40, choose from the articles A–D. The articles may be chosen more than once.

Mark your answers on the separate answer sheet.

The world of freelance work
Four writers look at the working life of freelancers

A

Anyone contemplating going freelance should bear in mind that to make a real go of it may well involve working harder than in an employed position. The life doesn't suit everyone and many employed people see freelancers as a totally different breed of worker, doing something that they couldn't do and wouldn't want to. Freelancers can find that they have less free time than they used to and that they take on more than they should out of a reluctance to turn down any offer. Furthermore, they may find themselves working for less money as they go along, as any rise in the number of freelancers in their field can drive fees down as a result of competition – some freelancers will be willing to accept low fees just to get work. There are dangers for companies too: using a large proportion of freelancers can mean that knowledge that is crucial to the company's operations lies outside the company itself.

B

As more and more people join the freelance workforce, it is perhaps time for an appraisal of this development. For the freelancers themselves, this means that a higher proportion of the working population consists of people who are free to decide on their own destinies, surely no bad thing. For companies, the development allows them ever-increasing flexibility, enabling them to adapt to changing circumstances quickly rather than having permanent staff who are underemployed at times. Freelance life, as anyone who does it knows well, is tough in some ways and to do well you need to be highly disciplined and organized, as well as hard-working and reliable – qualities that not everyone has when they are left to their own devices. A lot of employed people don't see things that way at all, tending to assume that freelancers have an easy life in which they can 'pick and choose' what they do, and may choose to do little.

C

An interesting by-product of companies relying on a significant number of freelancers is that a gap can open up between those freelancers and the employed personnel on the premises. This can be problematic, for example with key personnel in a project not on hand immediately if something urgent comes up. On the other hand, the increasing number of freelancers has big advantages for everyone involved, in a wide range of areas including flexible hours, child care arrangements and matching personnel to specific requirements. It is common for employed people to envy freelancers their perceived freedom compared to their own situation but this is largely a myth. To maintain a regular and viable income in freelance work takes effort and the equation is a simple one of effort and reward – your income depends on how hard you are prepared to work.

D

Freelancers often take more responsibility for their work than employed staff, who can become bored and demotivated, and in this regard it can be said that the more freelancers there are out there, the better it is for companies. To ensure the smooth running of this set-up, companies need to manage carefully their relationship with the freelance workforce – a coherent and mutually acceptable attitude needs to be developed for dealing with people who cannot be treated in the same way as permanent employees. For freelancers, making a sustainable career can be a nerve-racking business, as it can largely depend on chance encounters, word-of-mouth information from other freelancers and unexpected approaches from potential clients. It is this high-risk factor that puts many employees off the idea of going freelance.

Which writer

expresses a similar view to writer C on the consequences for companies of employing a
large number of freelancers? `37`

takes a different view from the others on the desirability of an increase in the number of
people becoming freelancers? `38`

takes the same view as writer B on the attitude of employed people to freelance work? `39`

has a different opinion from the others on the extent to which freelancers are in control of
how successful they become? `40`

TEST 4

You are going to read a newspaper article about a space programme. Six paragraphs have been removed from the article. Choose from the paragraphs **A–G** the one which fits each gap (**41–46**). There is one extra paragraph which you do not need to use.

Mark your answers on the separate answer sheet.

HOW I BECAME A BRITISH ASTRONAUT

May 18, 2009 was a sunny evening – a night that I have good cause to remember. I had recently retired from the Army Air Corps after an extremely rewarding career of nearly 18 years as a helicopter pilot and the future looked good – I'd been fortunate to secure a dream job working as a senior test pilot for a private firm. I had also just completed a year-long selection process for the European Astronaut Corps – an incredible experience that had opened my eyes to the world of human spaceflight.

41

A privately funded multimillion-dollar seat as a 'spaceflight participant' was unattainable for most. And opportunities such as the commercially sponsored Project Juno, which launched the first Briton, Helen Sharman, into space in 1989, were extremely rare.

42

This was designed to identify natural ability in various cognitive skills. In reality, this meant around eight hours of

individual computer-based exercises, becoming progressively harder and with only short breaks in between. Skills such as memory retention, concentration, spatial awareness and coordination were evaluated, alongside psychological questionnaires that were to become the benchmark of this selection process – hundreds of repetitive questions, aimed at ensuring consistency of answers over a long duration.

43

Historically, around 50 per cent of candidates fail the exacting medical requirements. Although good physical fitness is a strong attribute, the medical selection was not looking for potential Olympians. Instead, it was intended to select those individuals who pose the least risk of having a medical occurrence during their career. Space is no place to become ill.

44

As it happens, the medical selection caused exactly 50 per cent attrition, with failure to meet cardiovascular and eyesight

requirements being the two main causes. Having endured the most gruelling week of my life, I was delighted to be among the 22 remaining candidates.

45

The remainder of the selection process consisted of formal interviews, culminating in the final 10 being invited to meet ESA's Director General, Jean-Jacques Dordain. That was one month before that sunny evening in 2009, and I wondered who the lucky few would be. I suspected that I would not be one of them: an ESA press release had already announced that the new candidates would be presented at ESA headquarters in Paris on Wednesday. It was Monday night, I had not been contacted and time was getting tight.

46

This was a decision that would affect not just me but also my family. Thankfully, there was no time to dwell – I had to book a flight to Paris for the following day.

TEST 4

A It was also good to find that there were five British people in the group. Considering that, at the time, the UK was still in the shadow of a historical government policy not to participate in human spaceflight, it was encouraging to see the high level of interest regarding this astronaut selection.

B Other skills include being trained to perform spacewalks for external science and maintenance tasks and to manipulate the robotic arm in order to capture and berth visiting resupply vehicles. Then there is the medical training, communications skills training, emergency training – the list goes on.

C So when the phone rang and I was offered an opportunity to join the European Astronaut Corps, there was what can only be described as a wild mix of emotions – elation, excitement, shock and trepidation, due to an overwhelming realization that I was about to take my first steps down one of life's major forks in the road.

D It was interesting to meet the other candidates from all over Europe and to acknowledge the plethora of diverse career paths that had led us to this common goal. While it is fair to say that the best chances of success are to have a solid foundation in the core sciences or experience as a pilot, there really is no single route to becoming an astronaut – it has more to do with being passionate about what you do and being as good as you can be.

E Yet that situation changed when the European Space Agency (ESA) announced a selection for a new class of astronauts in 2008, and UK citizens were eligible to apply. My application joined the pile of nearly 10,000 others, and soon there followed an invitation to Hamburg to begin the testing process.

F During the previous five years working as a military test pilot, I had become much more involved in the space sector – aviation and space are intrinsically linked and share many similar technologies. However, I had not seriously contemplated a career as an astronaut, since the options to do so were extremely limited.

G Although the Soyuz spacecraft offers an emergency return to Earth in less than 12 hours from the International Space Station, this is an absolute last resort. Also, it is not available once a spacecraft has reached out beyond low Earth orbit.

You are going to read an article about the design of new stations on the London Underground railway system. For questions **47–56**, choose from the sections of the article (**A–E**). The sections may be chosen more than once.

Mark your answers *on the separate answer sheet*.

In which section of the article are the following mentioned?

the previously unattractive nature of the locations of most of the stations	**47**
a comparison Paoletti made to illustrate his approach to the JLE project	**48**
the immediate and massive effect that one of the stations had on its surroundings	**49**
a description that Paoletti considered not to be wholly accurate	**50**
a fundamental question concerning the function of stations in underground systems	**51**
an explanation Paoletti gave for why certain comments about the new buildings were incorrect	**52**
Paoletti's desire to unite elements that had previously been seen as wholly different from each other	**53**
personal qualities that enabled Paoletti to tackle the JLE project successfully	**54**
parts of a station architects were not responsible for in the past	**55**
Paoletti's opinion of those previously responsible for designing stations	**56**

TEST 4

Roland Paoletti *An architect who revolutionized the lives of London's commuters*

A Roland Paoletti was the driving force behind the dramatic, award-winning stations on the £3 billion Jubilee Line Extension (JLE) to the London Underground system, the most ambitious building programme on the Tube for many decades. An irascible Anglo-Italian, Paoletti possessed the persuasiveness and tenacity to take on the vested political interests at play in the planning of the 10-mile Jubilee Line Extension to ensure good design and innovation. Historically, architects employed on Tube projects had been restricted to 'fitting out' the designs of railway and civil engineers with few or no aesthetic concerns, and whom Paoletti dismissed as visionless 'trench-diggers'. The Jubilee line would be unique in that for the first time the architects would be responsible for designing entire underground stations.

B As the commissioning architect in overall charge, Paoletti's approach was to let light flood down into the stations along the line. The project's centrepiece was the extraordinary huge new station at Canary Wharf, designed by Norman Foster and Partners to handle up to 40,000 passengers an hour at peak times. 'Everybody keeps saying that it's like a cathedral,' complained Paoletti. 'They're wrong. It actually is a cathedral.' Explaining his approach to designing underground stations, Paoletti likened the Jubilee line to architectural free-form jazz, the stations responding to their different contexts as dramatic variations on a theme. Instead of uniformity, Paoletti envisaged variety achieved in the beauty of raw materials like concrete, and the

architectural power of simple, large spaces for robust and practical stations.

C He procured the most talented individual architects he could find to design 11 new stations along the line, creating a unique variety of architectural statement pieces – notably different but all beautiful – in what had been a largely desolate stretch of urban east London. 'For the price of an underground ticket,' he promised, 'you will see some of the greatest contributions to engineering and architecture worldwide.' Paoletti's sweeping vision did not disappoint. With their swagger and individualism, the stations have been widely acclaimed as a tour de force in public transport architecture.

D In pressing for a seamless marriage between architecture and engineering, Paoletti was concerned to make the stations pleasing to the eye, and the daily grind of commuters using them as uplifting an experience as possible. The result was generally reckoned to be the finest set of stations since the classic designs for the

Piccadilly line by Charles Holden in the 1930s. In Holden's day, design stopped at the top of the escalators leading down to the platforms, a symptom of the Tube's tradition of treating architecture and engineering as separate disciplines. From the start Paoletti promised 'a symbiosis of architecture and engineering' throughout. This is particularly evident at Westminster station, where Michael Hopkins solved structural difficulties by designing fantastic supporting structures redolent of science-fiction – what Paoletti called 'engineering that expresses itself as architecture ... in which people can delight'.

E He wanted the designs of the JLE stations to have a uniformity of voice, or, as he put it, 'a philosophical uniformity'. Paoletti contrasted the drama of MacCormac Jamieson Prichard's design for Southwark station with the vast glass drum of Ron Herron's Canada Water station, intended as a response to the area's bleakness, 'a big, splendid beacon that has transformed the area from a wasteland almost overnight'. To critics who complained about the expense of these grand designs, Paoletti pointed out that the same cut-and-cover, box-station design that allowed his architects a free hand with their various structures also saved London Underground millions in tunnelling costs. 'In any case,' he noted, 'you have to decide at the beginning whether you're going to see an underground station as a kind of vehicular underpass that happens to have people in it, or whether it's a building; a building with some other kind of job to do, like making people comfortable.'

Writing (1 hour 30 minutes)

PART 1

*You **must** answer this question. Write your answer in 220–260 words in an appropriate style.*

1   You have listened to a radio discussion programme about what can be done to increase participation in sports by people of all ages. You have made the notes below.

> Ways of increasing participation in sports
> - facilities
> - famous sportspeople
> - advertising

> Some opinions expressed in the discussion:
>
> 'What people need to get started in sports is enough free or cheap facilities.'
>
> 'Campaigns involving famous sportspeople are very effective because they are role models for young people.'
>
> 'If people know what is available to them, more of them might take up sports.'

Write an essay for your tutor discussing **two** of the ways in your notes. You should **explain which way you think is likely to be the most effective** for increasing participation in sports and **provide reasons** to support your opinion.

You may, if you wish, make use of the opinions expressed in the discussion, but you should use your own words as far as possible.

Write an answer to one of the questions 2–4 in this part. Write your answer in 220–260 words in an appropriate style.

2   You see this advertisement in an English-language magazine.

Festival Staff Required

We are looking for staff for an international rock festival, taking place over a three-day period in the west of England during the summer. We are looking for people with a good command of English who could work in the following areas:
- catering (food and drink stalls and tents)
- security (in the performance area, at entrances and around the site)
- first aid (for minor medical problems)
- retail (stalls selling merchandise relating to the artists appearing)

To apply, explain why you would like to work at the festival, give details of the role(s) you would prefer and why, and give reasons why you would be suitable. Send applications to the address below.

Write your **letter**.

3   A group of English-speaking visitors is going to come to the place where you work or study for a day next month. You have been asked to propose a programme for the day of their visit. In your proposal, you should suggest a schedule for the day, and give details of what each part of the schedule would involve from the beginning to the end of the visit.

Write your **proposal**.

4   As part of a class project about education and work, you have been asked to write a report on what young people in your city, region or country do after they leave school. Your report should include information about further studies that some young people do after they leave school and the kind of jobs that other young people do immediately after leaving school, and you should also mention where you got the information from.

Write your **report**.

TEST 4

Listening (40 minutes)

PART 1

You will hear three different extracts. For questions 1–6, choose the answer (A, B or C) which fits best according to what you hear. There are two questions for each extract.

Extract one
You hear two people talking.

1 What is the situation?
   A They have treated someone unfairly.
   B They have fallen out with someone.
   C They have changed their view of someone.

   [ ] 1

2 How do the speakers feel about the situation?
   A resigned
   B distressed
   C puzzled

   [ ] 2

Extract two
You hear two people on the radio discussing a letter from a listener.

3 What is the first speaker doing when he speaks?
   A suggesting that a problem is common
   B expressing sympathy about someone's problem
   C giving an objective account of a problem

   [ ] 3

4 The second speaker suggests that Paul should
   A accept that some people are unkind to others.
   B change his own attitude towards certain people.
   C confront the people who have upset him.

   [ ] 4

Extract three
You hear two people talking about jokes and comedy.

5 The first speaker says that punchlines
   A come in jokes that have formal structures.
   B tend to be funnier than catchphrases.
   C are easier to understand than in-jokes.

   [ ] 5

6 The second speaker says that many professional comedians
   A try to cause events that they can make jokes about.
   B exaggerate events that have actually happened to them.
   C become confused about what is fact and what is fiction.

   [ ] 6

You will hear part of a talk about a play. For questions 7–14, complete the sentences.

THE SHORT GOODBYE

The play was set in an [**7**] in Britain in the 1950s.

The main characters in the play worked for a company that produced
[**8**] .

An unusual feature of the play was that both main characters had a
[**9**] .

The main characters talked a lot about [**10**] of the time.

The man wanted to get an education and then have a career as a
[**11**] .

The woman wanted to earn a living from her ability at [**12**] .

One unusual feature of the set for the play was a [**13**] near the front of the stage.

Another unexpected feature was that there were several [**14**] at the back of the stage.

TEST 4

PART 3

You will hear a radio interview with a chef about the process of eating. For questions 15–20, choose the answer (A, B, C or D) which fits best according to what you hear.

15 Heston mentions eating fish from a paper plate with a plastic knife and fork
   A because it is something listeners may have done.
   B because doing so made him think about the process of eating.
   C as an example of an unpleasant eating experience.
   D as an example of what influences the eating experience.

15

16 What does Heston say about taste?
   A Fat should be considered a taste.
   B Taste and flavour are separate from each other.
   C The sense of smell is involved in it.
   D The number of taste buds gradually decreases.

16

17 The experiment involving salt and other food shows that
   A it is possible to taste something that you can't smell.
   B the sense of smell is not as powerful as other senses.
   C food can taste better when you can't smell it.
   D the flavour of food can change as you eat it.

17

18 The story about the trainee waiters illustrates that
   A certain colours are more appealing than others.
   B something can seem to taste good because of its appearance.
   C one sense can strongly influence another.
   D some people can perceive taste better than others.

18

19 What does Heston say about bitterness?
   A It can give a false impression that something is harmful.
   B It can become the main reason why people like something.
   C Reactions to it can change over time.
   D Its function is widely misunderstood.

19

20 The problem with the dish Heston describes was caused by
   A its appearance.
   B the taste of it.
   C its combination of flavours.
   D the fact that people ate it repeatedly.

20

PART 4

You will hear five short extracts in which people are talking about well-known individuals.

Task one

For questions 21–25, choose from the list A–H who each speaker is talking about.

A a coach

B a novelist

C a sportsman

D a journalist

E a businessman

F a TV newsreader

G a politician

H an actor

Speaker 1	21
Speaker 2	22
Speaker 3	23
Speaker 4	24
Speaker 5	25

Task two

For questions 26–30, choose from the list A–H each speaker's view of the person.

While you listen you must complete both tasks.

A scary

B underrated

C amusing

D unintelligent

E weird

F sincere

G lucky

H unpredictable

Speaker 1	26
Speaker 2	27
Speaker 3	28
Speaker 4	29
Speaker 5	30

TEST 4

Speaking (15 minutes)

PART 1 (2 minutes)

- Where do you work / study?
- How long have you been working/studying there?
- How important is it for people from your country to learn English?
- How much opportunity do you have to practise English outside of studying it?

- Would you like to do a different job / study something else? ..... (Why? / Why not?)
- Do you prefer to stay in or go out for entertainment? ..... (Why?)
- Do you spend a lot of time looking at screens? (Why / Why not?)
- What do you consider to be success in life? ..... (Why?)
- Do you prefer playing or watching sports? ..... (Why?)
- Which place in the world would you most like to visit? (Why?)
- Do you have a lot of friends or a small circle of close friends?
- Which TV programme(s) do you watch regularly? (Why?)

PART 2 (4 minutes)

1 **Interaction**
2 **Different surroundings**

Candidate A	Look at the three photographs 1A, 1B and 1C on page 91. They show **people interacting with each other.**
	Compare two of the photographs and say **what kind of people they might be, and what the situation might be.**
	Candidate A talks on his / her own for 1 minute.
Candidate B	**Which of the pictures reminds you most of a good or bad experience you've had?**
	Candidate B talks on his / her own for about 30 seconds.
Candidate B	Look at the three photographs 2A, 2B and 2C on page 91. They show **people in different surroundings.**
	Compare two of the photographs and say **why the people might be in the surroundings, and what kind of people they might be.**
	Candidate B talks on his / her own for 1 minute.
Candidate A	**Which of the surroundings would you most like to be in, and why?**
	Candidate A talks on his / her own for about 30 seconds.

TEST 4

PART 2

- What kind of people do you think they are?
- What do you think the situation might be?

1A

1B

1C

- Why do you think the people might be in these surroundings?
- What kind of people do you think they might be?

2A

2B

2C

TEST 4

PART 3 (4 minutes) and PART 4 (5 minutes)

The media

PART 3

Look at page 93, where there are some topics that are widely covered in the media.

Talk to each other about **how much influence coverage of these topics in the media has on people in general.**

Candidates A and B discuss this together for about 2 minutes.

Now decide **which topic is most influential for people in general by coverage of it in the media.**

Candidates A and B discuss this together for about 1 minute.

PART 4

- Some people say that the media does more harm than good. Do you agree?
- In what area(s) of life has the media had a good influence and in what area(s) has it had a bad influence?
- What would you like to see more coverage of in the media? (Why?)
- In some countries, a great many young people want to work in the media. Why do you think this is?
- To what extent do you believe what you are told by the media? To what extent do other people believe what they are told by the media?
- What developments in the media do you think might happen in the future?

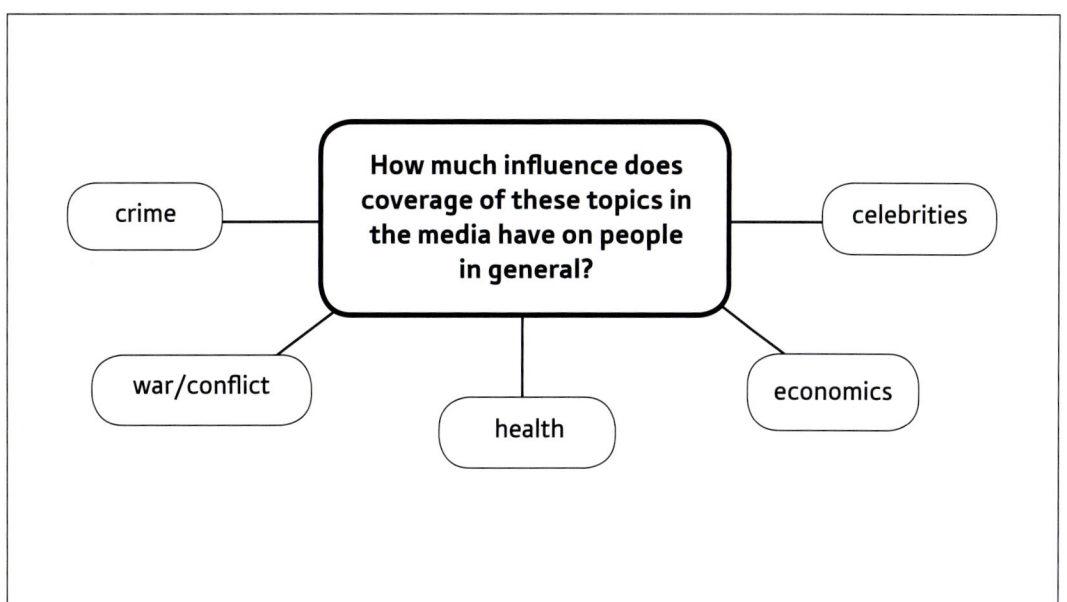

Cambridge English: Advanced Practice Test 1

Name ....

READING AND USE OF ENGLISH

PART 1: Mark ONE letter for each question.

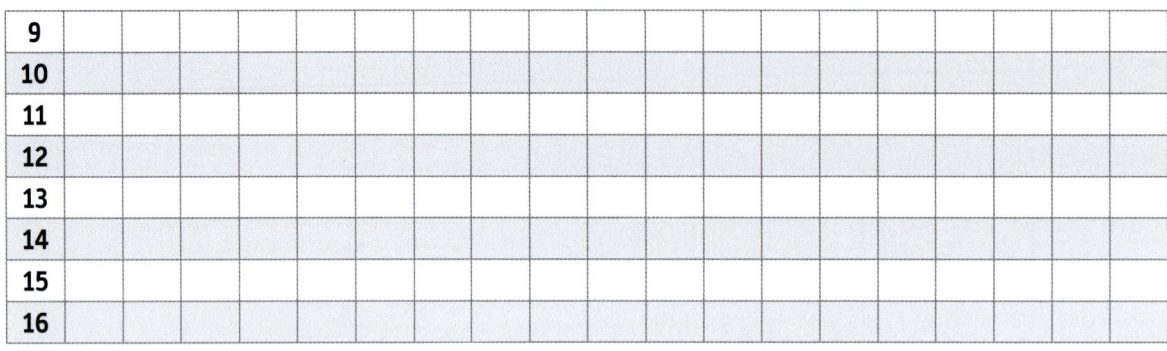

	A	B	C	D		A	B	C	D		A	B	C	D		A	B	C	D
1					3					5					7				
2					4					6					8				

PART 2: Write your answers clearly IN CAPITAL LETTERS. Write one letter in each box.

9	
10	
11	
12	
13	
14	
15	
16	

PART 3: Write your answers clearly IN CAPITAL LETTERS. Write one letter in each box.

17	
18	
19	
20	
21	
22	
23	
24	

PART 4: Write only the missing words IN CAPITAL LETTERS.

25	
26	
27	
28	
29	
30	

PART 5: Mark ONE letter for each question.

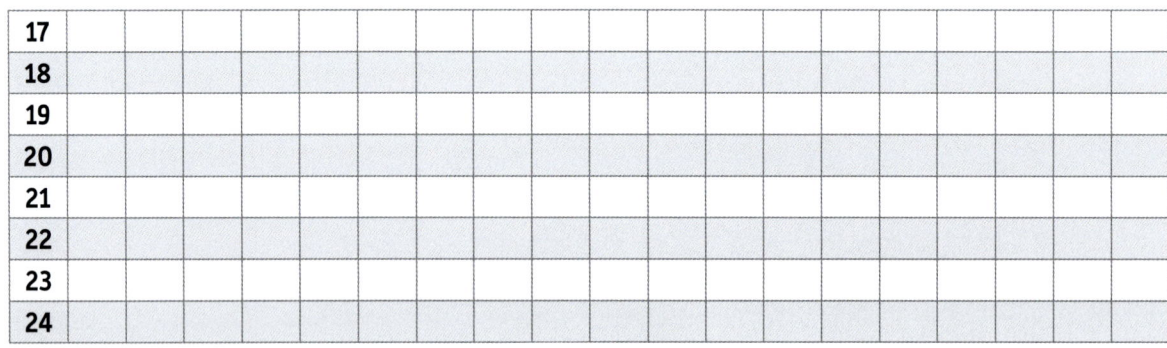

	A	B	C	D		A	B	C	D
31					34				
32					35				
33					36				

PART 6: Mark ONE letter for each question.

	A	B	C	D
37				
38				
39				
40				

PART 7: Mark ONE letter for each question.

41	A	B	C	D	E	F	G
42	A	B	C	D	E	F	G
43	A	B	C	D	E	F	G

44	A	B	C	D	E	F	G
45	A	B	C	D	E	F	G
46	A	B	C	D	E	F	G

PART 8: Mark ONE letter for each question.

47	A	B	C	D	E
48	A	B	C	D	E
49	A	B	C	D	E
50	A	B	C	D	E
51	A	B	C	D	E

52	A	B	C	D	E
53	A	B	C	D	E
54	A	B	C	D	E
55	A	B	C	D	E
56	A	B	C	D	E

LISTENING

PART 1: Mark ONE letter for each question.

1	A	B	C
2	A	B	C
3	A	B	C

4	A	B	C
5	A	B	C
6	A	B	C

PART 2: Write your answers clearly IN CAPITAL LETTERS. Write one letter in each box.

7																			
8																			
9																			
10																			
11																			
12																			
13																			
14																			

PART 3: Mark ONE letter for each question.

15	A	B	C	D
16	A	B	C	D
17	A	B	C	D
18	A	B	C	D
19	A	B	C	D
20	A	B	C	D

PART 4: Mark ONE letter for each question.

21	A	B	C	D	E	F	G	H
22	A	B	C	D	E	F	G	H
23	A	B	C	D	E	F	G	H
24	A	B	C	D	E	F	G	H
25	A	B	C	D	E	F	G	H
26	A	B	C	D	E	F	G	H
27	A	B	C	D	E	F	G	H
28	A	B	C	D	E	F	G	H
29	A	B	C	D	E	F	G	H
30	A	B	C	D	E	F	G	H

Cambridge English: Advanced   Practice Test 2

Name ....

READING AND USE OF ENGLISH

PART 1: Mark ONE letter for each question.

| 1 | A B C D | 3 | A B C D | 5 | A B C D | 7 | A B C D |
| 2 | A B C D | 4 | A B C D | 6 | A B C D | 8 | A B C D |

PART 2: Write your answers clearly IN CAPITAL LETTERS. Write one letter in each box.

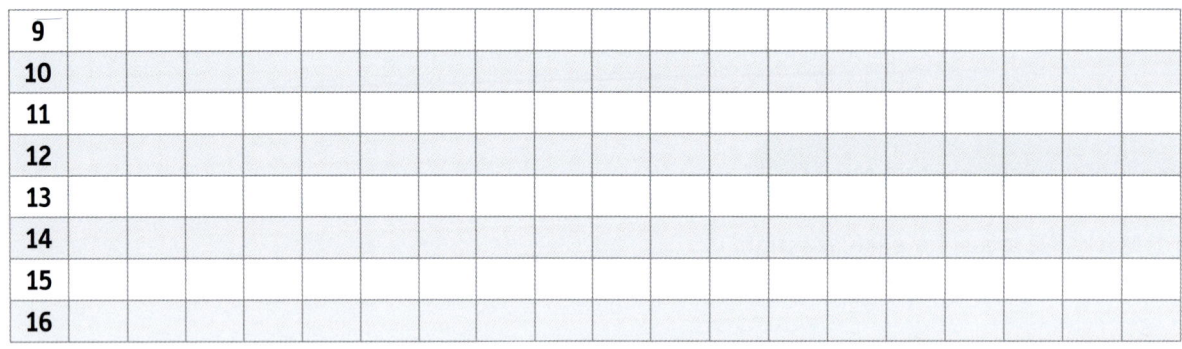

9	
10	
11	
12	
13	
14	
15	
16	

PART 3: Write your answers clearly IN CAPITAL LETTERS. Write one letter in each box.

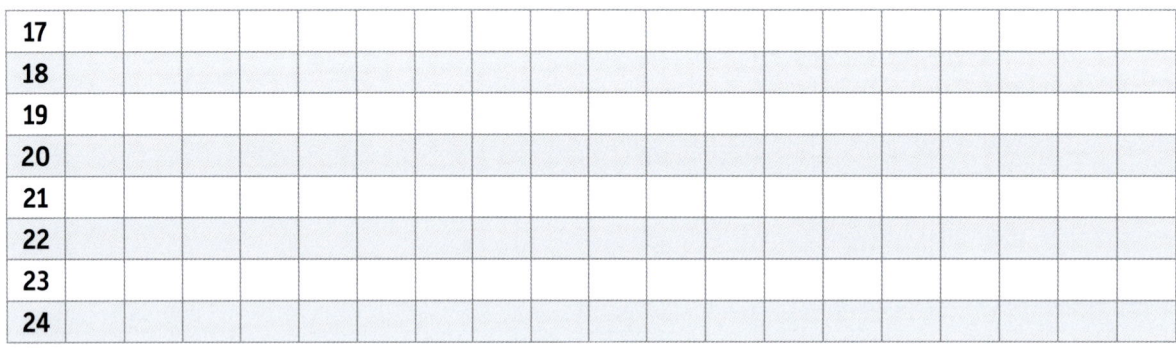

17	
18	
19	
20	
21	
22	
23	
24	

PART 4: Write only the missing words IN CAPITAL LETTERS.

25	
26	
27	
28	
29	
30	

PART 5: Mark ONE letter for each question.

31	A B C D
32	A B C D
33	A B C D

34	A B C D
35	A B C D
36	A B C D

PART 6: Mark ONE letter for each question.

37	A B C D
38	A B C D
39	A B C D
40	A B C D

PART 7: Mark ONE letter for each question.

41	A	B	C	D	E	F	G
42	A	B	C	D	E	F	G
43	A	B	C	D	E	F	G

44	A	B	C	D	E	F	G
45	A	B	C	D	E	F	G
46	A	B	C	D	E	F	G

PART 8: Mark ONE letter for each question.

47	A	B	C	D	E
48	A	B	C	D	E
49	A	B	C	D	E
50	A	B	C	D	E
51	A	B	C	D	E

52	A	B	C	D	E
53	A	B	C	D	E
54	A	B	C	D	E
55	A	B	C	D	E
56	A	B	C	D	E

LISTENING

PART 1: Mark ONE letter for each question.

1	A	B	C
2	A	B	C
3	A	B	C

4	A	B	C
5	A	B	C
6	A	B	C

PART 2: Write your answers clearly IN CAPITAL LETTERS. Write one letter in each box.

7	
8	
9	
10	
11	
12	
13	
14	

PART 3: Mark ONE letter for each question.

15	A	B	C	D
16	A	B	C	D
17	A	B	C	D
18	A	B	C	D
19	A	B	C	D
20	A	B	C	D

PART 4: Mark ONE letter for each question.

21	A	B	C	D	E	F	G	H
22	A	B	C	D	E	F	G	H
23	A	B	C	D	E	F	G	H
24	A	B	C	D	E	F	G	H
25	A	B	C	D	E	F	G	H
26	A	B	C	D	E	F	G	H
27	A	B	C	D	E	F	G	H
28	A	B	C	D	E	F	G	H
29	A	B	C	D	E	F	G	H
30	A	B	C	D	E	F	G	H

Cambridge English: Advanced Practice Test 3

Name ....

READING AND USE OF ENGLISH

PART 1: Mark ONE letter for each question.

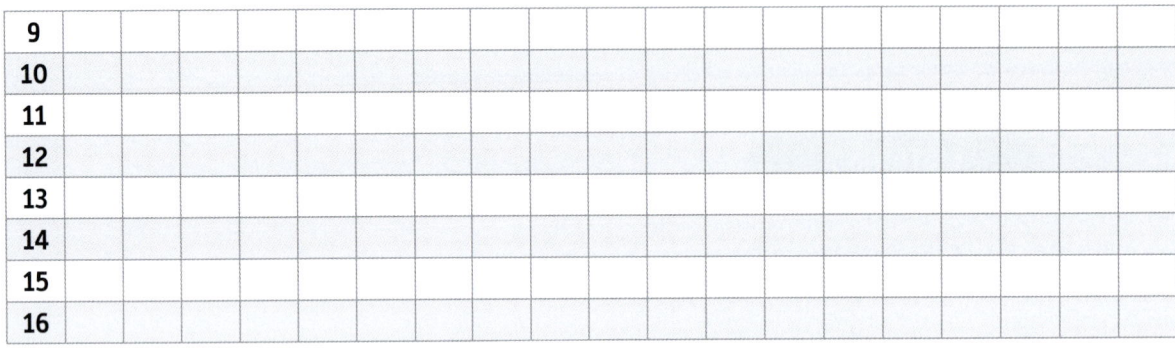

PART 2: Write your answers clearly IN CAPITAL LETTERS. Write one letter in each box.

9																		
10																		
11																		
12																		
13																		
14																		
15																		
16																		

PART 3: Write your answers clearly IN CAPITAL LETTERS. Write one letter in each box.

17																		
18																		
19																		
20																		
21																		
22																		
23																		
24																		

PART 4: Write only the missing words IN CAPITAL LETTERS.

25	
26	
27	
28	
29	
30	

PART 5: Mark ONE letter for each question.

31	A	B	C	D
32	A	B	C	D
33	A	B	C	D

34	A	B	C	D
35	A	B	C	D
36	A	B	C	D

PART 6: Mark ONE letter for each question.

37	A	B	C	D
38	A	B	C	D
39	A	B	C	D
40	A	B	C	D

PART 7: Mark ONE letter for each question.

41	A	B	C	D	E	F	G
42	A	B	C	D	E	F	G
43	A	B	C	D	E	F	G

44	A	B	C	D	E	F	G
45	A	B	C	D	E	F	G
46	A	B	C	D	E	F	G

PART 8: Mark ONE letter for each question.

47	A	B	C	D	E
48	A	B	C	D	E
49	A	B	C	D	E
50	A	B	C	D	E
51	A	B	C	D	E

52	A	B	C	D	E
53	A	B	C	D	E
54	A	B	C	D	E
55	A	B	C	D	E
56	A	B	C	D	E

LISTENING

PART 1: Mark ONE letter for each question.

1	A	B	C
2	A	B	C
3	A	B	C

4	A	B	C
5	A	B	C
6	A	B	C

PART 2: Write your answers clearly IN CAPITAL LETTERS. Write one letter in each box.

7	
8	
9	
10	
11	
12	
13	
14	

PART 3: Mark ONE letter for each question.

15	A	B	C	D
16	A	B	C	D
17	A	B	C	D
18	A	B	C	D
19	A	B	C	D
20	A	B	C	D

PART 4: Mark ONE letter for each question.

21	A	B	C	D	E	F	G	H
22	A	B	C	D	E	F	G	H
23	A	B	C	D	E	F	G	H
24	A	B	C	D	E	F	G	H
25	A	B	C	D	E	F	G	H
26	A	B	C	D	E	F	G	H
27	A	B	C	D	E	F	G	H
28	A	B	C	D	E	F	G	H
29	A	B	C	D	E	F	G	H
30	A	B	C	D	E	F	G	H

Cambridge English: Advanced   Practice Test 4

Name ....

READING AND USE OF ENGLISH

PART 1: Mark ONE letter for each question.

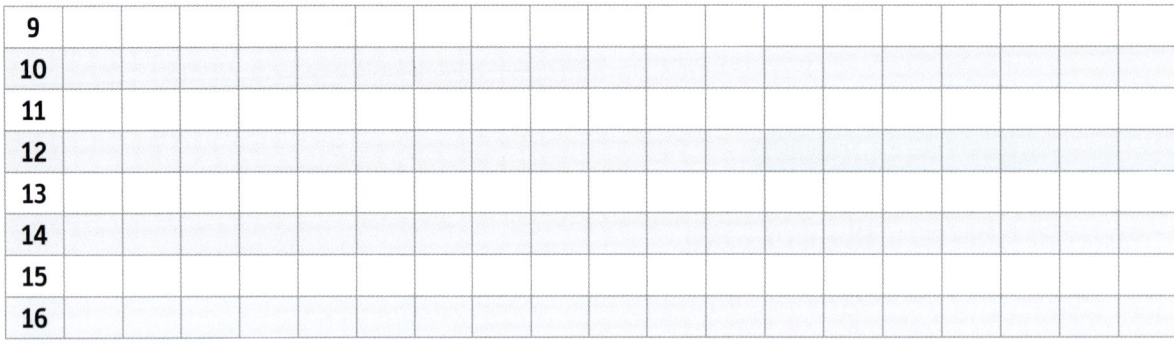

PART 2: Write your answers clearly IN CAPITAL LETTERS. Write one letter in each box.

9													
10													
11													
12													
13													
14													
15													
16													

PART 3: Write your answers clearly IN CAPITAL LETTERS. Write one letter in each box.

17													
18													
19													
20													
21													
22													
23													
24													

PART 4: Write only the missing words IN CAPITAL LETTERS.

25	
26	
27	
28	
29	
30	

PART 5: Mark ONE letter for each question.   **PART 6: Mark ONE letter for each question.**

	A	B	C	D			A	B	C	D			A	B	C	D
31	A	B	C	D		34	A	B	C	D		37	A	B	C	D
32	A	B	C	D		35	A	B	C	D		38	A	B	C	D
33	A	B	C	D		36	A	B	C	D		39	A	B	C	D
												40	A	B	C	D

PART 7: Mark ONE letter for each question.

41	A	B	C	D	E	F	G
42	A	B	C	D	E	F	G
43	A	B	C	D	E	F	G

44	A	B	C	D	E	F	G
45	A	B	C	D	E	F	G
46	A	B	C	D	E	F	G

PART 8: Mark ONE letter for each question.

47	A	B	C	D	E
48	A	B	C	D	E
49	A	B	C	D	E
50	A	B	C	D	E
51	A	B	C	D	E

52	A	B	C	D	E
53	A	B	C	D	E
54	A	B	C	D	E
55	A	B	C	D	E
56	A	B	C	D	E

LISTENING

PART 1: Mark ONE letter for each question.

1	A	B	C
2	A	B	C
3	A	B	C

4	A	B	C
5	A	B	C
6	A	B	C

PART 2: Write your answers clearly IN CAPITAL LETTERS. Write one letter in each box.

7															
8															
9															
10															
11															
12															
13															
14															

PART 3: Mark ONE letter for each question.

15	A	B	C	D
16	A	B	C	D
17	A	B	C	D
18	A	B	C	D
19	A	B	C	D
20	A	B	C	D

PART 4: Mark ONE letter for each question.

21	A	B	C	D	E	F	G	H
22	A	B	C	D	E	F	G	H
23	A	B	C	D	E	F	G	H
24	A	B	C	D	E	F	G	H
25	A	B	C	D	E	F	G	H
26	A	B	C	D	E	F	G	H
27	A	B	C	D	E	F	G	H
28	A	B	C	D	E	F	G	H
29	A	B	C	D	E	F	G	H
30	A	B	C	D	E	F	G	H

Assessing the Writing paper

Students' answers are assessed using a mark scheme which was developed with close reference to the Common European Framework of Reference for Languages (CEFR). Marks are awarded from 0 to 5 on each of the following four scales:

Content focuses on how well the candidate has fulfilled the task, in other words if they have done what they were asked to do.

Communicative achievement focuses on how appropriate the writing is for the task and whether the candidate has used the appropriate register.

Organization focuses on the way the candidate puts together the piece of writing, in other words if it is logical and ordered.

Language focuses on vocabulary and grammar. This includes the range of language as well as how accurate it is.

Tasks on the Cambridge English: Advanced Writing paper are assessed using the following scale, based on C1 of the CEFR:

C1	Content	Communicative achievement	Organization	Language
5	All content is relevant to the task. Target reader is fully informed.	Uses the conventions of the communicative task with sufficient flexibility to communicate complex ideas in an effective way, holding the target reader's attention with ease, fulfilling all communicative purposes.	Text is a well-organized, coherent whole, using a variety of cohesive devices and organizational patterns with flexibility.	Uses a range of vocabulary, including less common lexis, effectively and precisely. Uses a wide range of simple and complex grammatical forms with full control, flexibility and sophistication. Errors, if present, are related to less common words and structures, or occur as slips.
4	*Performance shares features of Bands 3 and 5.*			
3	Minor irrelevances and/or omissions may be present. Target reader is on the whole informed.	Uses the conventions of the communicative task effectively to hold the target reader's attention and communicate straightforward and complex ideas, as appropriate.	Text is well organized and coherent, using a variety of cohesive devices and organizational patterns to generally good effect.	Uses a range of vocabulary, including less common lexis, appropriately. Uses a range of simple and complex grammatical forms with control and flexibility. Occasional errors may be present but do not impede communication.
2	*Performance shares features of Bands 1 and 3.*			
1	Irrelevances and misinterpretation of task may be present. Target reader is minimally informed.	Uses the conventions of the communicative task to hold the target reader's attention and communicate straightforward ideas.	Text is generally well organized and coherent, using a variety of linking words and cohesive devices.	Uses a range of everyday vocabulary appropriately, with occasional inappropriate use of less common lexis. Uses a range of simple and some complex grammatical forms with a good degree of control. Errors do not impede communication.
0	Content is totally irrelevant. Target reader is not informed.	*Performance below Band 1*		

Assessing the Speaking paper

Assessment is based on performance in the whole test, and is not related to performance in particular parts of the test. Students are assessed on their own individual performance and not in relation to each other.

Marks are awarded by the assessor, who does not take part in the test, according to five analytical criteria: *Grammatical resource*, *Vocabulary resource*, *Discourse management*, *Pronunciation*, and *Interactive communication*. The interlocutor, who conducts the test, gives a mark for *Global achievement*.

C1	Grammar and vocabulary	Lexical resource	Discourse management	Pronunciation	Interactive communication
5	Maintains control of a range grammatical forms.	Uses a wide range of appropriate vocabulary to give an exchange views on familiar and unfamiliar topics.	Produces extended stretches of language with very little hesitation. Contributions are relevant, coherent and varied. Uses a wide range of cohesive devices and discourse markers.	Is intelligible. Phonological features are used effectively to convey and enhance meaning.	Initiates with ease, linking contributions to those of other speakers. Widens the scope of the interaction and negotiates towards an outcome.
4	*Performance shares features of Bands 3 and 5.*				
3	Shows a good degree of control of a range of simple and some complex grammatical forms.	Uses a range of appropriate vocabulary to give and exchange views on familiar and unfamiliar topics.	Produces extended stretches of language with very little hesitation. Contributions are relevant and there is a clear organization Uses a range of cohesive devices and discourse markers.	Is intelligible. Intonation is appropriate. Sentence and word stress is accurately placed. Individual sounds are articulated clearly.	Initiates and responds appropriately, linking contributions of those of other speakers. Maintains and develops the interaction and negotiates towards an outcome.
2	*Performance shares features of Bands 1 and 3.*				
1	Shows a good degree of control of simple grammatical forms and attempts some complex grammatical forms.	Uses appropriate vocabulary to give and exchange views, but only when talking about familiar topics.	Produces extended stretches of language with very little hesitation. Contributions mostly relevant and there is a clear organization of ideas. Uses a range of cohesive devices.	Is intelligible. Intonation is generally appropriate. Sentence and word stress is generally accurately placed. Individual sounds are generally articulated clearly.	Initiates and responds appropriately. Maintains and develops the interaction and negotiates towards an outcome with very little support.
0	*Performance below Band 1.*				

C1	Global achievement
5	Handles communication on a wide range of topics, including unfamiliar and abstract ones, with very little hesitation. Uses accurate and appropriate linguistic resources to express complex ideas and concepts and produce extended discourse that is coherent and easy to follow.
4	*Performance shares features of Bands 3 and 5.*
3	Handles communication on a range of familiar and unfamiliar topics, with very little hesitation. Uses accurate and appropriate linguistic resources to express ideas and produce extended discourse that is generally coherent.
2	*Performance shares features of Bands 1 and 3.*
1	Handles communication on familiar topics, despite some hesitation. Organizes extended discourse but occasionally produces utterances that lack coherence, and some inaccuracies and inappropriate usage occur.
0	*Performance below Band 1.*